365 DAYS OF AIR FRYER COOKBOOK

EMMA KATIE

Check out more books by Emma Katie at:
www.amazon.com/author/emmakatie

CONTENTS

Breakfast Recipes

Lunch Recipes

Dinner Recipes

Snacks Recipes

Dessert Recipes

1 INTRODUCTION

The idea of deep frying without using oil or with minimum oil has hit the market with great success. It's quite problem solving for those of the potato chips or fried food lovers. Just like a deep fryer the food is placed into a basket and then unlike frying in oil food is heated by air stream all over and around the basket. There's a simple thermostat to set cooking temperature and a rotary timer to set time. It automatically turns off once done. You can use basket divider to cook more than one food at a time.

Having an air fryer means you can have all your favorite fried foods without using oil. For example air fried chicken, crisp on outside and moist on inside. Likewise, stuffed vegetables, when you fry them in oil they absorb lots of oil which is not the case with air fried stuffed vegetables. You can fry them without any oil and the result is even more delicious. These are just examples, the list of recipes and choices is limitless in this book.

History of Air Fryer
Official use of air fryer dates back in 2010 when Australia and Europe first launched it. Afterwards, the word approached America and Japan too. And now it has become an important kitchen gadget all over the world.

How Does Air Fryer Works?
The technology an air fryer uses to cook food is Rapid Air Technology. With this technology the air is circulated on high degrees, up to 200°C, to "air fry" any food such as fish, chicken or chips etc. This technology has brought a new era of cooking by deep frying with up to 80% less fat as compared to old-fashioned deep fat frying.

In air fryer cooking heat is released through a heating element which cooks the food more appropriately. There's an exhaust fan too right above the cooking chamber that provides the food required airflow. This way food is cooked with constant heated air. As a result, the same heating temperature reaches every part of the food cooking. So this is only grill and the exhaust fan that helps the air fryer to boost air at a constantly high speed to cook healthy food with least fat.

The internal pressure increases the temperature that is then controlled by exhaust system. Exhaust fan also emits filtered extra air to cook the food healthier way. Air fryer is completely odorless and harmless making it user and environment friendly.

Cooling System in Air Fryer
Where there is a heating system in air fryer there is a cooling system too with a fan placed on motor axis that controls the internal temperature. This cooling fan is to ensure the clean and healthy food. Hence the internal parts of an air fryer are cooled from top to bottom through fresh air.

Benefits of Air Fryer

Wondering how an air fryer can benefit you? Here are some of many reasons to buy your own air fryer.

- Uses no or least oil
- Time saving
- One pot cooking without creating mess in kitchen
- Easy to operate
- Cooks scrumptious food
- Cooks healthy food
- Cooks a limitless variety of foods
- Cooks frozen food too
- Cooks two to three items at a time using divider

Air fryers don't only cook but most of them bake, grill, steam and roast as well. Make sure about your needs and the functions of air fryer before buying one.

Making a Pick for Best Air Fryer

- It's best to choose a brand with good reputation in market. Later on, you can also easily find their accessories.
- Consider the design; the color and the size should fit your kitchen interior.
- The one with easily removable accessories and easy to clean.
- Light weight is always easier to handle.
- Pick the one according to the capacity you need for your daily food. For smaller families choose the smaller one and vice versa for larger families. Selecting the one that suit your capacity would make your machine last longer and also save your electricity bill.
- Before buying do a quick market search for the prices, features and functions. If you're buying one that's more expensive with more features then make sure you need those features such as grill pan, baking dish or double layer rack.

Never forget that proper use and good maintenance would add life of any of your appliance.

Breakfast Recipes

Mushroom & Egg in a Cup

Time: 25 minutes   Servings: 2

Ingredients:

1 tablespoon olive oil
½ red onion, sliced thinly
2 cups button mushrooms, sliced thinly
3 eggs

Salt, to taste
Cooking spray, as required
3 tablespoons feta cheese, crumbled

Directions:

Preheat the Airfryer at 330 degrees F.
In a skillet, heat oil on medium heat.
Add onion and mushroom and sauté for about 5 minutes.
Transfer the mushroom mixture in a bowl and keep aside to cool.
In a small bowl, add eggs and salt and beat well.
Grease a 6-inch ramekin with cooking spray.
Place the eggs into prepared ramekin.
Place the mushroom mixture over the eggs and top with cheese.
Arrange the ramekin in Airfryer basket and cook for about 10-12 minutes or till done completely.

Bacon & Egg in a Cup

Time: 35 minutes   Servings: 2

Ingredients:

1 bacon slice
2 eggs
2 tablespoons milk
Freshly ground black pepper, to taste

1 teaspoon marinara sauce
1 tablespoon Parmesan cheese, grated
1 tablespoon fresh parsley, chopped
2 bread slices, toasted and buttered

Directions:

Preheat the Airfryer at 355 degrees F.
Place the bacon in Airfryer and cook for about 18 minutes or trill tender.
Remove from the Airfryer and cut into small pieces.
Divide the bacon in 2 ramekins.
Crack 1 egg in each ramekin over bacon.
Pour milk over eggs evenly and sprinkle with black pepper.
Top with marinara sauce, followed by the Parmesan cheese.
Cook for about 8 minutes or till desired doneness.
Sprinkle with parsley and serve alongside the toasts.

Ham, Spinach & Egg in a Cup

Time: 35 minutes   Servings: 4

Ingredients:

1 tablespoon unsalted butter, melted
1 tablespoon olive oil
1 pound fresh baby spinach
4 eggs

7-ounce ham, sliced
4 teaspoons milk
Salt and freshly ground black pepper, to taste

Directions:

Preheat the Airfryer to 355 degrees F.
Grease the 4 ramekins with butter.
In a skillet, heat oil on medium heat.
Add spinach and cook for about 2-3 minutes or till just wilted.
Drain the liquid completely from the spinach.
Divide the spinach into prepared ramekins, followed by ham slices.
Crack 1 egg into each ramekin over ham slices.
Drizzle with milk evenly and sprinkle with salt and black pepper.
Baked for 15 -20 minutes or till desired doneness of eggs.

Bacon, Tomato & Egg in a Cup

Time: 20 minutes   Servings: 2

Ingredients:

½ teaspoon butter
2 bread slices
1 bacon slice, chopped
4 tomato slices
1 tablespoon Mozzarella cheese, shredded
2 eggs

1/8 teaspoon maple syrup
1/8 teaspoon balsamic vinegar
¼ teaspoon fresh parsley, chopped
Salt and freshly ground black pepper, to taste
2 tablespoons mayonnaise

Directions:

Preheat the Airfryer to 320 degrees F.
Lightly, grease 2 ramekins.
Line each prepared ramekin with 1 bread slice.
Divide bacon and tomato slices over bread slice evenly in each ramekin.
Top with the cheese evenly.
Crack 1 egg in each ramekin over cheese.
Drizzle with maple syrup and balsamic vinegar and then sprinkle with parsley, salt and black pepper.
Arrange the ramekins in an Airfryer basket and cook for about 10 minutes or till desired doneness.
Top with mayonnaise and serve

Bacon, Bell Pepper & Egg in a Cup

Time: 25 minutes

Servings: 6

Ingredients:

6 bacon slices
6 bread slices
1 scallion, chopped

3 tablespoons green bell pepper, seeded and chopped
2 tablespoons mayonnaise
6 eggs

Directions:

Preheat the Airfryer to 375 degrees F.
Grease 6 cups muffin tin with cooking spray.
Line the sides of each prepared muffin cup with 1 bacon slice.
Cut bread slices with round cookie cutter.
Arrange the bread slice in the bottom of each muffin cup.
Place a slice of bacon into each muffin cup.
Top with, scallion, bell pepper and mayonnaise evenly.
Carefully, crack one egg in each muffin cup.
Cook for about 15 minutes or till eggs are done completely.
Serve warm.

Sausage in a Cup

Time: 35 minutes

Servings: 2

Ingredients:

¼ cup cream
3 eggs
2 cooked sausages, sliced

1 bread slice, cut into sticks
¼ cup mozzarella cheese, grated

Directions:

Preheat the Airfryer to 355 degrees F.
Grease 2 ramekins.
In a bowl, add cream and eggs and beat well.
Transfer the egg mixture into ramekins.
Place the sausage slices and bread sticks around the edges and gently push them in the egg mixture.
Sprinkle with the cheese evenly.
Place ramekins in Airfryer basket.
Cook for about 20-22 minutes or till desired doneness.

*E*GGS WITH SAUSAGE & BACON

Time: 25 minutes   Servings: 4

Ingredients:
8 bacon slices   Salt and freshly ground black pepper, to
8 chicken sausages   taste
4 eggs

Directions:
Preheat the Airfryer to 320 degrees F.
In an Airfryer basket, place bacon slices and sausages.
Cook for about 10 minutes.
Lightly, grease 4 ramekins.
Crack 1 egg in each prepared ramekin.
Sprinkle with salt and black pepper.
Cook for about 10 minutes.
Divide bacon slices and sausage in serving plates.
Place 1 egg in each plate and serve.

*E*GGS WITH MUSHROOM & HAM

Time: 25 minutes   Servings: 1

Ingredients:
½ cup shredded cheddar cheese   1 tablespoon salad greens
4 small button mushroom, quartered   1 egg
4 cherry tomatoes, halved   Salt and freshly ground black pepper, to
3 slices shaved ham   taste
½ sprig of rosemary, chopped   1 croissant

Directions:
Preheat the Airfryer at 355 degrees F.
Brush the oven proof dish with butter.
Spread the cheese in a bottom of the dish.
Top with mushrooms, tomatoes, ham slices, rosemary and salad greens.
Crack egg into the center.
Season with salt and pepper.
Place the dish and croissant in a fryer basket.
Cook the croissant for about 4 minutes.
Cook the egg dish for about 8 minutes.

SCRAMBLED EGGS

Time: 20 minutes   Servings: 2

Ingredients:
4 eggs
Salt and freshly ground black pepper, to taste
1 tablespoon butter

Directions:
Preheat the Airfryer at 285 degrees F.
In a bowl, add the eggs, salt and black pepper and beat well.
In a baking pan, melt butter and tilt the pan to spread the butter in the bottom.
Add the beaten eggs and cook for about 10 minutes, stirring occasionally.

SCRAMBLED EGGS WITH MUSHROOMS

Time: 20 minutes   Servings: 2

Ingredients:
4 eggs
Salt and freshly ground black pepper, to taste   ½ cup fresh mushrooms, chopped finely
2 tablespoons unsalted butter   2 tablespoons Parmesan cheese, shredded

Directions:
Preheat the Airfryer at 285 degrees F.
In a bowl, add the eggs, salt and black pepper and beat well.
In a baking pan, melt butter and tilt the pan to spread the butter in the bottom.
Add the beaten eggs and cook for about 4-5 minutes
Add the mushrooms and cheese and cook for 5 minutes, stirring occasionally.

SCRAMBLED EGGS WITH TOMATOES

Time: 20 minutes   Servings: 4

Ingredients:
¾ cup milk   8 grape tomatoes, halved
4 eggs   ½ cup Parmesan cheese, grated
Salt and freshly ground black pepper, to
taste

Directions:
Preheat the Airfryer to 355 degrees F.
Grease the Airfryer pan completely with cooking spray.
In a bowl, add milk, egg, salt and black pepper and beat well.
Transfer the egg mixture into the prepared pan.

Cook for about 6 minutes till edges begin to set.

With a wooden spatula, stir the egg mixture.

Top with tomatoes and cook for about 3 minutes or till the eggs are done.

Serve warm with the topping of cheese.

*S*IMPLE OMELET

Time: 20 minutes   Servings: 2

Ingredients:
3 eggs
2 tablespoons milk
1 teaspoon butter, melted

Salt and freshly ground black pepper, to taste

Directions:
Preheat the Airfryer to 355 degrees F.

Grease the Airfryer pan.

In a bowl, add all ingredients and beat well.

Pour egg mixture in prepared pan.

Cook for about 15 minutes or till done completely.

*O*NION OMELET

Time: 20 minutes
Serving: 1

Ingredients:
1 medium onion, sliced
2 eggs
1/8 teaspoon chives, minced

Dash of soy sauce
Freshly ground black pepper, to taste
1 tablespoon cheddar cheese, grated

Directions:
Preheat the Airfryer to 355degrees F.

Grease the Airfryer pan.

Add onion and cook for about 10 minutes.

Meanwhile in a bowl, add eggs, chives, soy sauce and black pepper and beat well.

Pour egg mixture over onion and sprinkle with cheese.

Cook for about 10 minutes or till done completely.

ZUCCHINI OMELET

Time: 25 minutes   Servings: 2

Ingredients:
1 teaspoon butter
1 zucchini, julienned
4 eggs
¼ teaspoon fresh basil, chopped

¼ teaspoon red pepper flakes, crushed
Salt and freshly ground black pepper, to taste

Directions:
Preheat the Airfryer to 355 degrees F.
In a skillet, melt butter on medium heat.
Add zucchini and cook for about 3-4 minutes.
In a bowl, add the eggs, basil, red pepper flakes, salt and black pepper and beat well.
Add cooked zucchini and gently, stir to combine.
Transfer the mixture into an Airfryer pan.
Cook for about 10 minutes or till done completely.

BACON & HOT DOGS OMELET

Time: 15 minutes   Servings: 2

Ingredients:
4 eggs
2 hot dogs, chopped

1 bacon slice, chopped
2 small onions, chopped

Directions:
Preheat the Airfryer to 320 degrees F.
In an Airfryer baking pan, crack the eggs and beat well.
Add remaining ingredients and gently, stir to combine.
Cook for about 10 minutes or till done completely.

HAM OMELET

Time: 40 minutes   Servings: 2

Ingredients:
4 small tomatoes, chopped
4 eggs
Salt and freshly ground black pepper, to taste

2 ham slices
1 onion, chopped

Directions:
Preheat the Airfryer to 390 degrees F.
Grease the Airfryer pan

Add the tomatoes and cook for about 10 minutes.
Meanwhile, heat a non-stick skillet on medium heat.
Add ham and onion and stir fry for about 4-5 minutes.
In a bowl, add the eggs, salt and black pepper and beat well.
After 10 minutes, set the Airfryer to 335 degrees F.
In the pan, add the beaten eggs and ham mixture and stir to combine.
Cook for about 20 minutes or till done completely.

PEPPERONI OMELET

Time: 20 minutes   Servings: 2

Ingredients:
3 eggs
2 tablespoons milk
Pinch of salt

Freshly ground black pepper, to taste
8-10 pepperoni slices

Directions:
Preheat the Airfryer to 355 degrees F.
In an Airfryer pan, crack the eggs and beat well.
Add remaining ingredients and gently, stir to combine.
Cook for about 10-12 minutes or till done completely.

CHICKEN OMELET

Time: 40 minutes   Servings: 2

Ingredients:
1 teaspoon butter
1 onion, chopped
½ of jalapeño pepper, seeded and chopped
3 eggs

Salt and freshly ground black pepper, to taste
¼ cup cooked chicken, shredded

Directions:
In a frying pan, melt butter on medium heat.
Add onion and sauté for about 4-5 minutes.
Add jalapeño pepper and sauté for about 1 minute.
Stir in chicken and remove from heat.
Preheat the Airfryer to 355 degrees F.
Grease the Airfryer pan.
Meanwhile in a bowl, add eggs, salt and black pepper and beat well.
Place the chicken mixture into prepared pan.
Pour egg mixture over chicken mixture.
Cook for about 10 minutes or till done completely.

Tofu Omelet

Time: 20 minutes   Servings: 2

Ingredients:

8-ounce silken tofu, pressed and sliced   ½ teaspoon olive oil
3 eggs   Freshly ground black pepper, to taste
2 teaspoons fish sauce   1 teaspoon corn flour
½ teaspoon sesame oil   2 teaspoons water

Directions:

Preheat the Airfryer to 390 degrees F.

Lightly, grease an Airfryer pan.

Place tofu in the bottom of prepared pan.

In a small bowl, dissolve corn flour into water.

In a large bowl, add corn flour mixture, eggs, fish sauce, both oils and black pepper and beat well.

Place the eggs mixture over tofu.

Cook for about 8-10 minutes or till done completely.

Spicy Tofu & Scallion Omelet

Time: 20 minutes   Servings: 2

Ingredients:

3 large eggs   Pinch of red pepper flakes, crushed
Dash of sesame oil   1 small tube Japanese tofu, cut into ½-inch
Dash of soy sauce   thick pieces
Pinch of ground coriander   ¼ cup scallion, chopped
Pinch of ground cumin   ¼ cup fresh cilantro, chopped

Directions:

Preheat the Airfryer to 390 degrees F.

In a bowl, ,add eggs, sesame oil, soy sauce, coriander, cumin and red pepper flakes and beat till well combined.

Lightly, grease an Airfryer pan.

Place tofu in the bottom of prepared pan.

Place scallion and cilantro over tofu evenly and top with egg mixture.

Cook for about 8-10 minutes or till done completely.

Tofu & Mushroom Omelet

Time: 35 minutes   Servings: 2

Ingredients:

2 teaspoons canola oil   1 garlic clove, minced
¼ of onion, chopped   8-ounce silken tofu, pressed and sliced

3½-ounce fresh mushrooms, sliced
Salt and freshly ground black pepper, to taste

3 eggs, beaten

Directions:

Preheat the Airfryer to 355 degrees F.

In an Airfryer pan, add the oil, onion and garlic and cook for about 4 minutes.

Add the tofu and mushrooms and sprinkle with salt and black pepper.

Place the beaten eggs on top evenly.

Cook for about 25 minutes, opening after every 8 minutes to poke the eggs.

CREAMY PARSLEY SOUFFLÉ

Time: 15 minutes

Servings: 2

Ingredients:

2 tablespoons light cream
2 eggs
1 tablespoon fresh parsley, chopped

1 fresh red chili pepper, chopped
Salt, to taste

Directions:

Preheat the Airfryer to 390 degrees F.

Grease 2 soufflé dishes.

In a bowl, add all ingredients and beat till well combined.

Transfer the mixture into prepared soufflé dishes.

Cook for about 8 minutes.

CARROT FRITTATA

Time: 45 minutes

Servings: 4

Ingredients:

2 tablespoons olive oil
3 medium carrots, peeled and chopped finely
1 leek, sliced thinly into rings
2 garlic cloves, minced

6 large eggs
Salt and freshly ground black pepper, to taste
1 teaspoon fresh parsley, minced
½ cup cheddar cheese, shredded

Directions:

In a large non-stick skillet, heat oil on medium heat.

Add carrots, leeks and garlic and cook for about 4-5 minutes, stirring occasionally.

Remove from heat and keep aside to cool slightly.

Add carrot mixture and stir to combine.

Preheat the Airfryer at 330 degrees F.

Grease a baking dish.

In a bowl, add egg, salt, black peppers and parsley and beat well.

Add mushroom mixture and stir to combine.
Place the egg mixture into prepared baking dish.
Spread cheddar cheese over egg mixture evenly.
Cook for about 30 minutes.

MIXED VEGGIES FRITTATA

Time: 30 minutes   Servings: 2

Ingredients:
2 bacon slices, chopped
4-6 cherry tomatoes, halved
¼ cup green bell pepper, seeded and
chopped

1 tablespoon olive oil
3 large eggs
¼ cup fresh spinach, chopped
¼ cup cheddar cheese, shredded

Directions:
Preheat the Airfryer to 360 degrees F.
In a baking dish, mix together bacon, tomatoes and bell pepper.
Cook for about 8 minutes.
Meanwhile in a bowl, add eggs, spinach and cheese and beat till well combined.
Pour the egg mixture over bacon mixture
Cook for about 8 minutes more.

MIXED VEGGIES & SAUSAGE FRITTATA

Time: 30 minutes   Servings: 4

Ingredients:
1 teaspoon butter
2 chorizo, sliced
½ cup fresh mushrooms, sliced
2 baby red potatoes, sliced thinly
1 red onion, sliced
8 eggs

1 tablespoon tomato paste
½ teaspoon paprika
Salt and freshly ground black pepper, to
taste
¾ cup Parmesan cheese, grated
¼ cup fresh parsley, chopped

Directions:
In a large non-stick skillet, melt butter on medium heat.
Add chorizo, mushrooms, potatoes and onion and cook for about 6-8 minutes, stirring occasionally.
Preheat the Airfryer to 340 degrees F.
In a bowl, add eggs, tomato paste, paprika, salt and black pepper and beat well.
In a small bowl, mix together cheese and parsley.
Place the vegetable mixture into a baking dish.
Place egg mixture over vegetable mixture.
Top with cheese mixture.
Cook for about 7 minutes.

MUSHROOMS FRITTATA

Time: 20 minutes   Servings: 2

Ingredients:

1 tablespoon butter
2 cups button mushrooms, cut into ½-inch thin slices
½ of red onion, cut into ½-inch thin slices

3 eggs
3 tablespoons feta cheese, crumbled
Salt and freshly ground black pepper, to taste

Directions:

In a skillet, melt butter on medium heat.
Add onion and mushroom and sauté for about 5 minutes.
Remove from heat and keep aside to cool.
Preheat the Airfryer to 390 degrees F.
Grease a large ramekin,
In a bowl, add the eggs, salt and black pepper and beat well.
Add egg mixture into prepared ramekin.
Top with mushroom mixture.
Cook for about 10-12 minutes.

CREAM CHEESE MUSHROOMS FRITTATA

Time: 45 minutes   Servings: 4

Ingredients:

1 shallot, sliced thinly
2 garlic cloves, minced
4 cups white mushrooms, chopped
2 tablespoons olive oil
6 large eggs

¼ teaspoon red pepper flakes, crushed
Salt and freshly ground black pepper, to taste
½ teaspoon fresh dill, minced
½ cup cream cheese, softened

Directions:

In a skillet, heat oil on medium heat.
Add shallot, mushrooms and garlic and sauté for about 5-6 minutes.
Remove from heat and keep aside to cool.
Preheat the Airfryer at 330 degrees F.
Grease a baking dish.
In a bowl, add egg, red pepper flakes, salt and black peppers and beat well.
Add mushroom mixture and stir to combine.
Place the egg mixture into prepared baking dish.
Sprinkle with dill.
Spread cream cheese over egg mixture evenly.
Cook for about 30 minutes.

Bacon & Mushrooms Frittata

Time: 25 minutes   Servings: 2

Ingredients:

1 tablespoon olive oil
1 bacon slice, chopped
6 cherry tomatoes, halved
6 fresh mushrooms, sliced
Salt and freshly ground black pepper, to taste

3 eggs
1 tablespoon fresh parsley, chopped
½ cup Parmesan cheese, grated and divided

Directions:

Preheat the Airfryer to 390 degrees F.
In a baking dish, mix together, bacon, tomatoes, mushrooms, salt and black pepper and bake for about 6 minutes.
In a bowl, add eggs and beat well.
Add parsley and half of the cheese and mix.
Pour the egg mixture over bacon mixture evenly and bake for about 8 minutes.

Sausage, Corn& Potato Frittata

Time: 20 minutes   Servings: 2

Ingredients:

1 tablespoon olive oil
½ of chorizo sausage, sliced
½ cup frozen corn
1 large potato, boiled, peeled and cubed
3 jumbo eggs

Salt and freshly ground black pepper, to taste
2 tablespoons feta cheese, crumbled
1 tablespoon fresh parsley, chopped

Directions:

Preheat the Airfryer at 355 degrees F.
In the pan of Airfryer, add the oil.
Add sausage, corn and potato and cook for 5-6 minutes or till golden brown.
In a small bowl, add the eggs, salt and black pepper and beat well.
Pour eggs over the sausage mixture and top with cheese and parsley
Cook for about 5 minutes or till desired doneness.

Sausage & Tomato Frittata

Time: 25 minutes   Servings: 2

Ingredients:

½ of Italian sausage
4 cherry tomatoes, halved

3 eggs
1 tablespoon Parmesan cheese, shredded

1 tablespoon olive oil
1 teaspoon fresh parsley, chopped

Salt and freshly ground black pepper, to taste

Directions:

Preheat the Airfryer to 360 degrees F.

In a baking pan, place the sausage and tomatoes.

Cook for about 5 minutes till done.

In a bowl, add eggs, cheese, oil, parsley, salt and black pepper and beat till well combined.

Remove baking dish and place egg mixture over sausage and tomatoes.

Cook for about 5 minutes or till desired doneness.

$\mathcal{P}$ANCETTA & SPINACH FRITTATA

Time: 15 minutes   Servings: 2

Ingredients:

¼ cup pancetta
½ tomato, cubed
¼ cup fresh baby spinach
3 eggs

Salt and freshly ground black pepper, to taste
¼ cup Parmesan cheese, grated

Directions:

Preheat the Airfryer to 355 degrees F.

Add pancetta and tomato and cook for about 5 minutes.

In a small bowl, add the eggs, salt and black pepper and beat well.

Pour eggs and cheese over the pancetta mixture.

Cook for about 5 minutes or till desired doneness.

$\mathcal{T}$ROUT FRITTATA

Time: 35 minutes   Servings: 4

Ingredients:

2 tablespoons olive oil
1 onion, sliced
6 eggs
½ tablespoon horseradish sauce

2 tablespoons crème fraiche
2 hot-smoked trout fillets
¼ cup fresh dill, chopped

Directions:

Preheat the Airfryer to 320 degrees F.

In a frying pan, heat oil on medium heat.

Add onion and sauté for about 4-5 minutes.

Meanwhile in a bowl, add eggs, horseradish sauce and crème fraiche and beat till well combined.

Transfer the onion mixture into a baking dish.

Top with egg mixture and trout.

Cook for about 20 minutes or till desired doneness.

CRUST-LESS TOMATO & ONION QUICHE

Time: 40 minutes   Servings: 2

Ingredients:
4 eggs   ½ cup milk
¼ cup onion, chopped   1 cup Gouda cheese, shredded
½ cup tomatoes, chopped   Salt, to taste

Directions:
Preheat the Airfryer to 340 degrees F.
In a ramekin, add all ingredients and mix till well combined.
Cook for about 30 minutes till fully cooked.

BACON QUICHE

Time: 45 minutes   Servings: 2

Ingredients:
½ cup all-purpose flour   Salt and freshly ground black pepper, to
2 tablespoons butter   taste
1 tablespoon water   ¼ cup cooked bacon, crumbled
1 cup whipping cream   ¼ cup cheddar cheese, shredded
2 eggs

Directions:
In a bowl, add flour.
With a pastry cutter, cut the butter till a soft clumpy mixture forms.
Add water and with your hands mix till a ball forms.
Place the dough ball into a small quiche pan and with your fingertips, press along the bottom and about
      ½-inch up the sides.
Preheat the Airfryer to 400 degrees F.
Arrange the quiche pan into an Airfryer basket.
Cook for about 10 minutes.
Meanwhile in a bowl, add whipping cream, eggs, salt and black pepper and beat till well combined.
Remove the quiche pan from Airfryer.
Spread bacon over crust evenly and top with cheese evenly.
Place egg mixture over cheese and bacon evenly.
Now, set the Airfryer to 360 degrees F.
Cook for about 22-25 minutes.

Ham & Mushroom Quiche

Time: 65 minutes   Servings: 3

Ingredients:

1 (9-inch) prepared pie dough (at room temperature)
1 tablespoon ghee
1-ounce button mushrooms, sliced
2 tablespoons ham, chopped
¼ cup onion, chopped

1/3 cup heavy cream
3 large eggs
½ teaspoon fresh thyme, chopped
Salt and freshly ground black pepper, to taste
½ cup Swiss cheese, grated

Directions:

Place the pie dough into an 8-invh pie plate and trim off the excess dough.

Line the pie dough with a parchment paper and add the pie weights.

Preheat the Airfryer to 400 degrees F.

Arrange the quiche pan into an Airfryer basket.

Cook for about 10 minutes.

Remove the pie pan from Airfryer.

Remove the pie weights and parchment paper from crust and keep aside to cool.

Meanwhile in a skillet, melt ghee on medium heat.

Add mushrooms and cook for about 4-5 minutes.

Add ham and onion and cook for about 4-5 minutes.

Transfer the ham mixture over cooled crust evenly.

In a bowl, add heavy cream, eggs, thyme, salt and black pepper and beat till well combined.

Place egg mixture over cheese and bacon evenly.

Now, set the Airfryer to 300 degrees F.

Cook for about 30 minutes.

Chicken & Broccoli Quiche

Time: 20 minutes   Servings: 9

Ingredients:

1 frozen ready-made pie crust
½ tablespoon olive oil
1 egg
1/3 cup cheddar cheese, grated
3 tablespoons whipping cream

Salt and freshly ground black pepper, to taste
¼ cup boiled broccoli, chopped
¼ cup cooked chicken, chopped

Directions:

Preheat the Airfryer to 390 degrees F.

Lightly, grease 2 small pie pans.

Cut 2 (5-inch) rounds from the dough.

Arrange the 1 dough round in each pie pan and press in the bottom and sides.

In a bowl, add egg, cheese, cream, salt and black pepper and beat till well combined.

Pour egg mixture over the dough base.

Top with broccoli and cheese evenly.

Arrange the pie pans into an Airfryer basket.

Cook for about 12 minutes.

*E*GGLESS SPINACH & BACON QUICHE

Time: 20 minutes   Servings: 4

Ingredients:

2 cooked bacon slices, chopped
½ cup fresh spinach, chopped
¼ cup mozzarella cheese, shredded
½ cup Parmesan cheese, shredded

2 tablespoons milk
2 dashes Tabasco sauce
Salt and freshly ground black pepper, to taste

Directions:

Preheat the Airfryer to 320 degrees F.

Grease a baking dish.

In a bowl, add all ingredients and mix well.

Transfer the mixture into prepared baking dish.

Cook for about 8 minutes.

*K*ALE QUICHE

Time: 40 minutes   Servings: 8

Ingredients:

For Crust

½ cup flour, sifted
3 tablespoons chilled unsalted butter
¼ teaspoon fine sugar
Salt and freshly ground black pepper, to taste
2-3 tablespoons cold water
1 egg, beaten

For Filling:

2½ tablespoons milk
2 eggs
½ teaspoon garlic, chopped finely
Pinch of freshly ground black pepper
½ cup fresh baby kale, chopped
¼ cup mozzarella cheese, shredded

Directions:

For crust in a chilled bowl, mix together all ingredients except water and egg.

Refrigerate the flour mixture for about 15 minutes.

Add cold water and mix till a dough forms.

Divide the dough into 2 equal sized portions.

Cover the dough and refrigerate for about 30 minutes.

Place each dough portion between 2 parchment papers.

Roll into a slightly thin crust larger than the pie pan.

Arrange the crusts in the bottom of 2 (5-inch) pie dishes.

Cut the extra dough.

With a fork, poke the crusts and coat with the beaten egg evenly.

Preheat the Airfryer to 320 degrees F.

Cook the crusts for about 8 minutes.

Remove from air fryer and keep aside.

For filling in a bowl, add eggs, milk, garlic and black pepper and beat till well combined.

Stir in kale.

Now, set the Airfryer to 335 degrees F.

Divide the egg mixture between both crusts.

Cook for about 10 minutes.

Remove the pie dishes from Airfryer and sprinkle with cheese evenly.

Cook for about 4 minutes more.

SALMON QUICHES

Time: 35 minutes   Servings: 2

Ingredients:

5½-ounce salmon fillet, chopped (5.5 oz.)
Salt and freshly ground black pepper, to taste
½ tablespoon fresh lemon juice
1 egg yolk
3½ tablespoons chilled butter

2/3 cup flour
1 tablespoon cold water
2 eggs
3 tablespoons whipping cream
1 scallion, chopped

Directions:

In a bowl, mix together salmon, salt, black pepper and lemon juice and keep aside.

In another bowl, add egg yolk, butter, flour and water and mix till a dough forms.

Place the dough onto a floured smooth surface and roll into about 7-inch round.

Place the dough in a quiche pan and press firmly in the bottom and along the edges.

Trim the excess edges.

In a small bowl, add the eggs, cream, salt and black pepper and beat till well combined.

Place the cream mixture over crust evenly.

Top with the chopped salmon, followed by the scallion.

Preheat the Airfryer to 355 degrees F.

Arrange the quiche pan in Airfryerbasket.

Cook for about 20 minutes.

Mini Macaroni Quiches

Time: 30 minutes   Servings: 4

Ingredients:

1 short crust pastry
½ cup leftover macaroni and cheese
2 tablespoons plain Greek yogurt
1 teaspoon garlic puree

11-ounce milk
2 large eggs
2 tablespoons Parmesan cheese, grated

Directions:

Dust 4 ramekins with a little flour.
Line the bottom of prepared ramekins with shortcrust pastry.
In a bowl, mix together macaroni, yogurt and garlic.
Transfer the macaroni mixture between ramekins about ¾ full.
In a small bowl, addmilk and egg and beat well.
Place the egg mixture over the macaroni mixture.
Top with the cheese evenly.
Preheat the Airfryer to 355 degrees F.
Arrange the ramekins in Airfryer basket.
Cook for about 20 minutes.

Ham Casserole

Time: 25 minutes   Servings: 2

Ingredients:

2 teaspoons unsalted butter, softened
2-ounce ham, sliced thinly
4 large eggs, divided
Salt and freshly ground black pepper, to taste

2 tablespoons heavy cream
1/8 teaspoon smoked paprika
3 tablespoons Parmesan cheese, grated finely
2 teaspoons fresh chives, minced

Directions:

Preheat the Airfryer to 320 degrees F.
Spread butter in the pie pan.
Place ham slices in the bottom of the pie pan.
In a bowl, add 1egg, salt, black pepper and cream and beat till smooth.
Place the egg mixture over the ham slices evenly.
Carefully, crack the remaining eggs on top.
Sprinkle with paprika, salt and black pepper.
Top with cheese and chives evenly.
Place the pie pan in an Airfryer and cook for about 12 minutes or till the egg are set.
Serve with toasted bread slices.

HAM & VEGGIE WITH EGGS

Time: 20 minutes   Servings: 2

Ingredients:

6 small button mushroom, quartered
6 cherry tomatoes, halved
4 slices shaved ham
2 tablespoons salad greens
1 cup cheddar cheese, shredded

2 eggs
1 tablespoon fresh rosemary, chopped
Salt and freshly ground black pepper, to taste
2 croissants

Directions:

Preheat the Airfryer to 320 degrees F.

Grease a baking dish with butter.

In a bowl, mix together the mushrooms, tomatoes, ham and greens.

Place half of the vegetable mixture in the prepared baking dish.

Top with the half of the cheese.

Repeat the layers once.

Make 2 wells in the mixture and carefully, crack the eggs in the wells.

Sprinkle with rosemary, salt and black pepper.

Place the baking dish and croissants in an Airfryer basket.

Cook the croissants for about 4 minutes and egg mixture for about 8 minutes,

SAUSAGE, BACON WITH VEGGIES

Time: 25 minutes   Servings: 4

Ingredients:

8 cherry tomatoes, halved
8 chestnut mushrooms
1 garlic clove, minced
1 teaspoon olive oil
Salt and freshly ground black pepper, to taste

4 smoked bacon rashers
4 chipolatas sausages
7-ounce fresh baby spinach
4 eggs

Directions:

Preheat the Airfryer to 390 degrees F.

In a round baking pan, add tomatoes, mushrooms and garlic.

Drizzle with oil and sprinkle with salt and black pepper.

Arrange the bacon and sausages in an Airfryer basket along alongside pan of veggies.

Cook for about 10 minutes.

Meanwhile in a sieve, place spinach.

Pour boiling water over spinach and drain well.

Remove the pan from Airfryer.

Place the spinach into pan over veggie mixture evenly.

Carefully, crack the eggs over the spinach.

Now, set the Airfryer at 320 degrees F.

Place the baking pan in an Airfryer basket.

Cook for about 8 minutes,

Divide the eggs and vegetables mixture in 4 serving plates.

Serve alongside bacon and sausages.

SAUSAGE & BACON WITH BEANS

Time: 30 minutes   Servings: 6

Ingredients:

6 bacon slices   1 can baked beans
6 medium sausages   6 bread slices, toasted
4 eggs

Directions:

Preheat the Airfryer at 320 degrees F.

Place the bacon and sausages in a fryer basket and cook for about 10 minutes.

In first ramekin, place the baked beans.

In another ramekin, place the eggs

Now, set the Airfryer to 390 degrees F.

Cook for about 10 minutes more.

Divide the sausage mixture, beans and eggs in 4 serving plates and serve alongside the bread slices.

SQUID WITH EGG

Time: 35 minutes   Servings: 4

Ingredients:

½ cup self-rising flour   2 green chilies, seeded and chopped
14-ounce flower squid, cleaned   2-3 curry leaves
Salt and freshly ground black pepper, to 4 raw salted egg yolks
taste   ½ cup chicken broth
1 tablespoon olive oil   2 tablespoons evaporated milk
2 tablespoons butter   1 tablespoon sugar

Directions:

Preheat the Airfryer to 355 degrees F.

Grease an Airfryer pan.

In a shallow dish, place the flour and keep aside.

Pat dry the flower squid with paper towel.

Sprinkle the flower squid with salt and black pepper evenly.

Coat the squid in flour evenly and then shake off any excess flour.

Place flower squid into prepared Airfryer pan and cook for about 9 minutes.

Remove from Airfryer and keep aside
In a skillet, heat oil and butter on medium heat.
Add chilies and curry leaves and cook for about 3 minutes.
Add egg yolks and cook, stirring for about1 minute.
Gradually, add the chicken broth and cook, stirring continuously for about 3-5 minutes.
Add milk and sugar and mix till well combine.
Add fried flower squid and toss in the sauce till evenly coated.

*V*EGGIE HASH

Time: 55 minutes   Servings: 4

Ingredients:
2 teaspoons butter
1 medium onion, chopped
½ of green bell pepper, seeded and chopped
1½ pound russet potatoes, peeled and cubed

1 teaspoon dried thyme, crushed
Salt and freshly ground black pepper, to taste
5 eggs

Directions:
Preheat the Airfryer to 390 degrees F.
In an Airfryer pan, melt the butter for about 1-2 minutes.
Add onion and bell pepper and cook for about 5 minutes.
Add the potatoes, herbs, salt and black pepper and cook for about 30 minutes.
Meanwhile, heat a greased skillet on medium heat.
Add the beaten eggs and cook for about 1 minute per side or till desired doneness.
Remove from the skillet and cut it into small pieces.
Add the egg pieces into Airfryer pan and cook for about 5 minutes more.

*M*IXED VEGGIE HASH

Time: 45 minutes   Servings: 4

Ingredients:
2 cups water
5 russet potatoes, peeled and cubed
½ tablespoon extra-virgin olive oil
½ of onion, chopped
½ jalapeño pepper, chopped
1 red bell pepper, seeded and chopped

¼ tablespoon dried oregano, crushed
1 teaspoon garlic powder
½ teaspoon ground cumin
¼ tablespoon red chili powder
Salt and freshly ground black pepper, to taste

Directions:
In a large bowl, add water and potatoes and keep aside for about 30 minutes.
Drain well and pat dry with the paper towel.

Preheat the Airfryer at 330 degrees F.

In a bowl, add the potatoes and oil and toss to coat well.

Place the potatoes into Airfryer basket and cook for about 5 minutes.

Transfer the potatoes onto a wire rack to cool.

In the same bowl, add remaining ingredients and toss to coat well.

Now, preheat the Airfryer to 390 degrees F.

Place the cooled potatoes into the bowl with veggie mixture and toss to coat well

Place the potato mixture in Airfryer basket and toss well.

Cook for about 15-20 minutes or till desired doneness.

Breakfast Burrito

Time: 25 minutes   Servings: 2

Ingredients:
2 eggs

Salt and freshly ground black pepper, to taste

2 whole-wheat tortillas

4-ounces cooked chicken breast slices

¼ of avocado, peeled, pitted and sliced

¼ of red bell pepper, seeded and sliced

2 tablespoon salsa

2 tablespoons mozzarella cheese, grated

Directions:
Preheat the Airfryer at 390 degrees F.

In a bowl, add the eggs, salt and pepper and beat well.

Place the beaten eggs in a small shallow nonstick pan.

Arrange the pan into an Airfryer basket and cook for about 5 minutes.

Remove egg from the pan.

Arrange the tortillas onto a smooth surface.

In each tortilla, divide the eggs, followed by chicken slice, avocado, bell pepper, salsa and cheese.

Roll up each tortilla tightly like a burrito.

Now, set the Airfryer at 355 degrees F.

Line an Airfryer tray with a foil paper.

Arrange the burrito in into prepared fryer tray.

Cook for about 3 minutes or till tortillas become golden brown.

French Toasts

Time: 15 minutes   Servings: 2

Ingredients:
2 eggs

¼ cup evaporated milk

3 tablespoons sugar

2 teaspoons olive oil

1/8 teaspoon vanilla extract

4 bread slices

Directions:

Preheat the Airfryer to 390 degrees F.

Grease the Airfryer pan and insert in the Airfryer while heating.

In a large shallow dish, add all the ingredients except the bread slices and beat till well combined.

Dip the each bread slice in egg mixture from both sides evenly.

Arrange the bread slices in the prepared pan.

Cook for about 2-3 minutes per side.

SAVOURY FRENCH TOASTS

Time: 15 minutes   Servings: 2

Ingredients:

¼ cup chickpea flour
3 tablespoons onion, chopped finely
2 teaspoons green chili, seeded and chopped finely
½ teaspoon red chili powder

¼ teaspoon ground turmeric
¼ teaspoon ground cumin
Salt, to taste
Water, as required
4 bread slices

Directions:

Preheat the Airfryer to 390 degrees F.

In a large bowl, add all the ingredients except the bread slices and mix till a thick mixture forms.

With a spoon, apply the mixture over the both sides of the bread slices.

Line the Airfryer pan with a foil paper.

Place the bread slices in the prepared pan.

Now, set the Airfryer to 355 degrees F.

Cook for about 3-4 minutes.

SPICED FRENCH TOAST STICKS

Time: 15 minutes   Servings: 2

Ingredients:

For Bread Sticks:
2 eggs
1/8 teaspoon ground cinnamon
Pinch of ground nutmeg
Pinch of ground cloves
Salt, to taste
4 bread slices

2 tablespoons butter, softened
Cooking spray, as required
For the Topping:
1 tablespoon icing sugar
2 tablespoons whipped cream
1 tablespoon maple syrup

Directions:

Preheat the Airfryer to 355 degrees F.

In a bowl, add eggs, cinnamon, nutmeg, cloves and salt and beat till well combined.

Spread the butter over both sides of the slices evenly.

Cut each bread slice into strips.
Dip bread strips into egg mixture evenly and place in Airfryer in 2 batches.
Cook for about 2 minutes and pause the Airfryer.
Transfer the pan onto a heat proof surface.
Coat the both sides of the bread strips with cooking spray.
Return the pan into Airfryer and cook for about 4 minutes.
Serve immediately with the topping of icing sugar, whipped cream and maple syrup.

$\mathcal{B}$UTTERED CINNAMON TOASTS

Time: 10 minutes   Servings: 6

Ingredients:

½ cup sugar
1½ teaspoons ground cinnamon
1½ teaspoons vanilla extract

¼ teaspoons freshly ground black pepper
½ cup salted butter, softened
12 whole wheat bread slices

Directions:

Preheat the Airfryer to 400 degrees F.
In a bowl, mix together sugar, vanilla, cinnamon, pepper and butter till smooth.
Spread butter mixture over each bread slice evenly.
Place the bread slices in an Airfryer basket.
Cook for about 5 minutes or till crispy.
Cut the bread slice diagonally and serve.

$\mathcal{S}$ALMON TOAST

Time: 20 minutes   Servings: 4

Ingredients:

4 bread slices
1 garlic clove, minced
8-ounce ricotta cheese
1 teaspoon lemon zest

4-ounce smoked salmon
1 shallot, sliced
1 cup arugula
Freshly ground black pepper, to taste

Directions:

Preheat the Airfryer to 355 degrees F.
Arrange the bread slices in an Airfryer basket.
Cook for about 5 minutes or till toasted.
In a food processor, add garlic, ricotta, lemon zest and pulse till smooth.
Spread ricotta mixture over each bread slice.
Top with salmon, shallot and arugula.
Sprinkle with black pepper and serve.

PICKLED TOASTS

Time: 25 minutes

Servings: 2

Ingredients:

4 bread slices, toasted
2 tablespoons unsalted butter, softened

2 tablespoons Branston pickle
¼ cup Parmesan cheese, grated

Directions:

Preheat the Airfryer to 390 degrees F.
Place the bread slice in a fryer basket.
Cook for about 5 minutes or till toasted.
Spread butter over bread slices evenly, followed by Branston pickle.
Top with cheese evenly.
Cook for about 4-5 minutes till cheese melts completely.

CHEESY MUSTARD TOASTS

Time: 20 minutes

Servings: 2

Ingredients:

4 bread slices
2 tablespoons cheddar cheese, shredded
2 eggs, whites and yolks, separated

1 tablespoon mustard
1 tablespoon paprika

Directions:

Preheat the Airfryer to 355 degrees F.
Place the bread slice in a fryer basket.
Cook for about 5 minutes or till toasted.
In a bowl, add egg whites and beat till soft peaks form.
In another bowl, add cheese, egg yolks, mustard and paprika and beat till well combined.
Gently, fold in egg whites.
Spread the mustard mixture over toasted bread slices.
Cook for about 10 minutes.

GARLICKYROLLS

Time: 15minutes

Servings: 2

Ingredients:

2 dinner rolls
½ cup Parmesan cheese, grated

2 tablespoons unsalted butter, melted
Garlic bread seasoning mix

Directions:

Preheat the Airfryer at 355 degrees F.
Cut the dinner rolls into cross style, but not the all way through.

Stuff the slits with the cheese evenly.

Coat the tops of each roll with butter.

Sprinkle with the seasoning mix evenly.

Cook for about 5 minutes or till cheese melts completely.

$\mathcal{P}$OTATO ROSTI

Time: 15minutes   Servings: 2

Ingredients:

1 teaspoon olive oil

½ pound russet potatoes, peeled and grated roughly

1 tablespoon chives, chopped finely

Salt and freshly ground black pepper, to taste

2 tablespoons sour cream

3.5 ounces smoked salmon, cut into slices

Directions:

Preheat the Airfryer to 355 degrees F.

Grease a pizza pan with the olive oil.

In a large bowl, add potatoes, chives, salt and black pepper and mix till well combined.

Place the potato mixture into the prepared pizza pan.

Arrange the pizza pan in an Airfryer basket.

Cook for about 15 minutes or till top becomes golden brown.

Cut the potato rosti into wedges.

Top with the sour cream and smoked salmon slices and serve immediately.

$\mathcal{P}$UMPKIN PANCAKES

Time: 20 minutes   Servings: 9

Ingredients:

3 tablespoons pumpkin filling

1 square puff pastry

1 small egg, beaten

Directions:

Preheat the Airfryer to 355 degrees F.

Roll out a square of puff pastry and layer it with pumpkin pie filling, leaving about ¼-inch space around the edges.

Cut it up into 9 equal sized square pieces.

Cover the gaps with beaten egg. 5.

Arrange the squares into a baking dish.

Cook for about 12 minutes.

Zucchini Fritters

Time: 20 minutes   Servings: 2

Ingredients:

300 g zucchini, grated and squeezed
200 g 1. Coarsely grate the zucchini and squeeze out as much liquid as possible in your hands. Also coarsely grate the cheese.
2. Combine zucchini, dill, cheese, flour, eggs. Salt & pepper to season.
3. Form fritters (using heaped teaspoon of the mixture) and Airfry in batches. Suggest 180 degree for around 6-7 min.
4. Top each fritter with 1/2 teaspoon yoghurt and a small sprig of dill.Halloumi cheese
30 g all-purpose flour
2 eggs
1 teaspoon fresh dill, minced
Salt and freshly ground black pepper, to taste
Plain yogurt, as required

Directions:

In a bowl, mix together all ingredients except yogurt.
Make small sized fritters from the mixture.
Preheat the Airfryer to 355 degrees F.
Grease a baking pan
Cook for about 6-7 minutes.
Topeach fritter with a dollopof yogurt and serve.

Egg & Bacon Sandwich

Time: 25 minutes   Servings: 2

Ingredients:

2 eggs, divided   2 English muffins, divided
Salt and freshly ground black pepper, to   2 bacon slices, divided
taste

Directions:

Crack 1 egg in an oven proof small bowl.
Season with salt and pepper.
Place the egg, 1 muffin and 1 bacon slice in an Airfryer.
Set the Airfryer to 390 degrees F.
Cook for about 5 minutes till done.
Repeat with the remaining ingredients.
Place egg over one slice of muffin.
Top with bacon and cover with another slice of muffin to make a sandwich.

SIMPLE CHEESE SANDWICHES

Time: 10 minutes   Servings: 2

Ingredients:
4 bread slices   4 teaspoons butter
4 American cheese slices

Directions:
Preheat the Airfryer to 370 degrees F.
Arrange 2 cheese slices between 2 bread slices.
Spread 2 teaspoons of butter over the both outsides of sandwich.
Repeat with the remaining slices, cheese and butter.
Arrange the sandwiches in an Airfryer basket.
Cook for about 8 minutes, flipping once in the middle way.

CHEESY TOMATO SANDWICH

Time: 10 minutes   Servings: 2

Ingredients:
4 bread slices   Salt and freshly ground black pepper, to
2 Swiss cheese slices   taste
8 tomato slices   4 teaspoons margarine

Directions:
Preheat the Airfryer to 355 degrees F.
Arrange 1 cheese slice over 1 bread slice.
Top with 2 tomato slices and sprinkle with salt and black pepper.
Cover with another 1bread slice.
Repeat with the remaining bread slices, cheese, tomato, salt and black pepper.
Arrange the sandwiches in an Airfryer basket.
Cook for about 5 minutes.
Remove sandwiches from Airfryer.
Spread 2 teaspoons of margarine over the both outsides of sandwich.
Cook for about 1 minute more.

CHEESY PROSCIUTTO & TOMATO SANDWICH

Time: 10 minutes   Servings: 2

Ingredients:
4 bread slices   1 teaspoon butter, melted
4 prosciutto slices   Salt and freshly ground black pepper, to
4 mozzarella cheese slices   taste

4 tomato slices   1 teaspoon fresh basil leaves, minced

Directions:
Preheat the Airfryer to 390 degrees F.
Arrange 1 cheese slice over 1 bread slice.
Top with 2 prosciutto slices and 2 cheese slices.
Cover with another 1bread slice.
Repeat with the remaining bread slices, cheese, tomato, salt and black pepper.
Arrange the sandwiches in an Airfryer basket.
Cook for about 5 minutes.
Remove sandwiches from Airfryer.
Place 2 tomato slices in each sandwich and sprinkle with salt and black pepper.
Drizzle with melted butter and serve,

TOASTED BAGELS

Time: 10 minutes   Servings: 6

Ingredients:
2 bagels, halved   Direction:
4 teaspoons butter
Preheat the Airfryer to 370 degrees F.
Arrange the bagels into an Airfryer basket.
Cook for about 3 minutes.
Remove the bagels from Airfryer.
Spread butter over bagels evenly.
Cook for about 3 minutes more.

CREAM BREAD

Time: 2 hours   Servings: 12

Ingredients:
1 cup milk   2 tablespoons milk powder
¾ cup whipping cream   1 teaspoon salt
1 large egg   ¼ cup fine sugar
4½ cups bread flour   3 teaspoons dry yeast
½ cup all-purpose flour

Directions:
Grease 2 bread tins.
In a bread machine, add all ingredients in the order listed above.
Set the dough function.
After the dough has finished its kneading cycle ad let it proof inside the machine for 45-50 minutes.
Remove the dough from pan.

Shape the dough into 4 equal sized balls.

Place each onto lightly floured surface and roll in a rectangle shape.

Tightly, roll each rectangle like a Swiss roll.

Place 2 rolls into each prepared bread tin.

Keep aside for about 1 hour.

Preheat the Airfryer at 375 degrees F.

Place the bread tins in Airfryer.

Cook for about 50-55 minutes.

SUNFLOWER SEEDS BREAD

Time: 40 minutes   Servings: 4

Ingredients:

2/3 cup whole wheat flour   ½ sachet instant yeast
2/3 cup plain flour   1 teaspoon salt
1/3 cup sunflower seeds   2/3-1 cup lukewarm water

Directions:

In a bowl, mix together flours, sunflower seeds, yeast and salt.

Slowly, add water, stirring continuously till a soft ball like dough forms.

Place the dough onto a lightly floured surface and with your hands, knead for about 5 minutes.

Make a ball from the dough and place into a bowl.

With a plastic wrap, cover the bowl and keep in warm place for about 30 minutes.

Preheat the Airfryer at 390 degrees F.

Coat the top of dough with water.

Arrange the dough into a greased cake pan.

Arrange the cake pan into an Airfryer basket.

Cook for about 18 minutes.

BANANA BREAD

Time: 35 minutes   Servings: 10

Ingredients:

1½ cupsself-risingflour   2 medium eggs
¼ teaspoonbicarbonate of soda   3½-ouncewalnuts, chopped
5 tablespoons plus 1 teaspoonbutter   2 cups bananas, peeled and mashed
2/3 cup plus ½ tablespooncaster sugar

Directions:

Preheat the Airfryer to 355 degrees F.

Grease a bread tin.

In a bowl, mix together flour andbicarbonate of soda.

In another bowl, add the butter and sugar and beat till pale and fluffy.

Add the eggs, one at a time along with a little flour and mix well.
Stir in the remaining flour and walnuts.
Add the mashed bananas and mix till well combined.
Transfer the mixture into the prepared tin.
Cook for about 10 minutes.
Now, set the Airfryer to 340 degrees F.
Cook for about 15 minutes.

NUTTY STILTON BUNS

Time: 25 minutes   Servings: 4

Ingredients:

3½ tablespoons butter, cubed   1/3 cup stilton
1/3 cup plain flour   ¼ cup walnuts, chopped

Directions:

In a food processor, add all ingredients and pulse till a dough forms.
Place the dough onto a lightly floured surface and roll into a log.
Wrap the log in a Clingfilm and freeze for about 30 minutes.
Preheat the Airfryer to 355 degrees F.
Line an Airfryer basket with a parchment paper.
Cut the dough into about 1/3-inch rounds.
Arrange the rounds into prepared basket.
Cook for about 15 minutes.

LEMONY BUNS

Time: 25 minutes   Servings: 12

Ingredients:

For Buns: **For Topping:**
3½-ounce butter   3½ tablespoons butter
5 tablespoons caster sugar   1 cup icing sugar
½ teaspoon vanilla essence   1 tablespoon fresh lemon juice
2 medium eggs   1 teaspoon fresh lemon rind, grated finely
2/3 cup self-rising flour   1 teaspoon dried cherries

Directions:

Preheat the Airfryer to 340 degrees F.
In a bowl, add butter and sugar and beat till light and fluffy.
Add the vanilla essence and ix well.
Add the eggs, one at a time with a little flour and eat till well combined.
Gently fold in remaining flour.
Fill the little bun cases with the mixture evenly.

Preheat the Airfryer to 340 degrees F.
Arrange the bun cases in batches in Airfryer.
Cook for about 8 minutes.
For topping in a bowl, add the butter and beat till creamy.
Slowly, add the icing sugar, beating continuously.
Stir in lemon juice and rind.
Remove the buns from the Airfryer.
Cut the buns in half.
Spread the lemon mixture over each half.
Top with cherries and serve,

UMPKIN BUNS

Time: 45 minutes   Servings: 15

Ingredients:

For Buns:

1 1/3 cups plus 1½ tablespoonsall-purpose flour
1½ tablespoons sugar
5 tablespoons milk
1/3 egg

1 teaspoon instant yeast
½ teaspoon salt
1-ounce butter, melted

For Egg Wash:

1 egg yolk
1 tablespoon milk

Directions

In a large bowl, add all ingredients, except the butter and mix till a smooth and elastic dough forms.
Add butter and mix till well combined.
With a mixer on low setting, mix the dough for at least 30 minutes.
With cling wrap, cover the dough and keep in warm place for about 2¾ hours.
Divide the dough into 15 equal sized buns.
For egg wash in a small bowl, mix together egg yolk and milk.
Brush the top of buns with egg wash.
With cling wrap, cover the buns and keep in warm place for about 45 minutes.
Preheat the Airfryer to 320 degrees F.
Arrange the buns onto baking dish.
Cook for about 5 minutes.

POTATO STUFFED BREAD ROLLS

Time: 65 minutes   Servings: 4

Ingredients:

5 large potatoes
2 tablespoons oil, divided
½ teaspoon mustard seeds

2 small onions, chopped finely
2 sprigs curry leaves
½ teaspoon ground turmeric

Salt, to taste

2 green chilies, seeded and chopped finely

2 tablespoons fresh cilantro, chopped finely

8 bread slices, trimmed

Directions:

In a large pan of salted water, add potatoes on medium heat and bring to a boil.

Cook for about 20-25 minutes or till potatoes are fork tender.

Drain well and peel the potatoes.

With a potato masher, mash the potatoes.

In a large skillet, heat 1 tablespoon of the oil on medium heat.

Add mustard seeds and sauté for about 30 seconds.

Add onions and sauté for about 4-6 minutes.

Add curry leaves and turmeric and sauté for about 30 seconds.

Add the mashed potatoes and salt and mix till well combined.

Remove from the heat and transfer into a bowl, then keep aside to cool.

After cooling, add chilies and cilantro and mix well.

Divide the mixture into 8 equal-sized portions

Shape each portion into an oval patty.

Wet the bread slices with water, one by one and with your palms, squeeze the moisture completely.

Place one patty in the center of each bread slice.

Roll the bread around the patty and seal the edges to secure the filling.

Coat the rolls with the remaining oil evenly.

Preheat the Airfryer at 390 degrees F.

Grease the Airfryer basket with some oil.

Place the rolls into the prepared basket and cook for about 12-13 minutes or till golden crisp.

VANILLA MUFFINS

Time: 25 minutes

Servings: 4

Ingredients

1 egg

3 egg yolks

2½ tablespoons plus 2 teaspoons sugar, divided

¼ teaspoon salt

2½ tablespoons vegetable oil

Few drops of vanilla paste

5 tablespoons cake flour, sifted

3 egg whites

Directions:

Preheat the Airfryer to 345 degrees F.

In a bowl, add egg, egg yolks, 2 teaspoons of the sugar and salt and beat till well combined.

Add oil and vanilla paste and beat till well combined

Add flour and mix till a smooth mixture forms.

In a small bowl, add egg whites and beat till frothy

Slowly, add remaining sugar and beat till stiff peaks form.

Fold in ¼ of the meringues into the egg yolk mixture.

Fold in remaining the meringue lightly in two portions till well combined.

Now, set the Airfryer at 285 degrees F.

Grease 4 muffin molds.

Transfer the mixture into prepared muffin molds evenly.

Cook for about 15 minutes or till a toothpick inserted in the center comes out clean.

Remove the muffin molds from Airfryer and keep on wire rack to cool for about 10 minutes.

Carefully turn on a wire rack to cool completely before serving.

ANANA MUFFINS

Time: 35 minutes   Servings: 12

Ingredients:

1 2/3 cups plain flour

1 teaspoon baking soda

1 teaspoon baking powder

1 teaspoon ground cinnamon

1 teaspoon salt

4 ripe bananas, peeled and mashed

2 eggs

½ cup brown sugar

1 teaspoon vanilla essence

3 tablespoon milk

1 tablespoon Nutella

¼ cup walnuts

Directions:

In a large bowl, sift together flour, baking soda, baking powder, cinnamon and salt.

In another bowl, add remaining ingredients except walnuts and beat till well combined.

Add the banana mixture into flour mixture and mix till just combined.

Fold in walnuts.

Preheat the Airfryer to 248 degrees F

Grease 12 muffin molds.

Transfer the mixture into prepared muffin molds evenly.

Cook for about 20-25 minutes or till a toothpick inserted in the center comes out clean.

Remove the muffin molds from Airfryer and keep on wire rack to cool for about 10 minutes.

Carefully turn on a wire rack to cool completely before serving.

APPLE MUFFINS

Time: 35 minutes   Servings: 12

Ingredients:

1¾ cups plain flour

1/3 cup white sugar

1½ teaspoons baking powder

½ teaspoon ground cinnamon

¼ teaspoon ground ginger

¼ teaspoon salt

¾ cup milk

1/3 cup applesauce

1 cup apple, cored and chopped

Directions:

In a large bowl, mix together, flour, sugar, baking powder, spices and salt.

Add milk and applesauce and beat till just combined.

Fold in chopped apple.

Preheat the Airfryer to 390 degrees F.

Grease 12 muffin molds.

Transfer the mixture into prepared muffin molds evenly.

Cook for about 20-25 minutes or till a toothpick inserted in the center comes out clean.

Remove the muffin molds from Airfryer and keep on wire rack to cool for about 10 minutes.

Carefully turn on a wire rack to cool completely before serving.

LEMONY RASPBERRY MUFFINS

Time: 35 minutes   Servings: 8

Ingredients:

¾ cup plus 2 tablespoons self-rising flour
½ teaspoon baking powder
Pinch of salt
½ cup plus 1 tablespoon butter, softened
5 tablespoons cream cheese, softened

½ cup caster sugar
2 eggs
2 teaspoonsfresh lemon juice
16 fresh raspberries

Directions:

In a bowl, mix together flour, baking powder and salt.

In another bowl, add butter and cream cheese and beat till light and creamy.

Add the caster sugar and beat till light and fluffy.

Add the eggs, one at a time and beat till well combined.

Add flour mixture into egg mixture and mix till just combined.

Stir in lemon juice.

Preheat the Airfryer to 365 degrees F.

Grease 8 muffin molds.

Transfer the mixture into prepared muffin molds evenly.

Top each cup with 2 raspberries.

Cook for about 20 minutes or till a toothpick inserted in the center comes out clean.

Remove the muffin moldstin from Airfryer and keep on wire rack to cool for about 10 minutes.

Carefully turn on a wire rack to cool completely before serving.

CITRUS BLUEBERRY MUFFINS

Time: 25 minutes   Servings: 12

Ingredients:

2 cups plus 2 tablespoons self-rising flour
5 tablespoons white sugar
½ cup milk
2-ounce butter, melted
2 eggs

2 teaspoons fresh orange zest, grated finely
2 tablespoons freshorange juice
½ teaspoon vanilla extract
½ cup fresh blueberries
Brown sugar, for sprinkling

Directions:

In a bowl, mix together flour and white sugar.

In another bowl, add remaining ingredients except blueberries and beat till well combined.

Add egg mixture into flour mixture and mix till well combined.

Fold in blueberries.

Preheat the Airfryer to 355 degrees F.

Grease 12 muffin molds.

Transfer the mixture into prepared muffin molds evenly.

Cook for about 12 minutes or till a toothpick inserted in the center comes out clean.

Remove the muffin molds from Airfryer and keep on wire rack to cool for about 10 minutes.

Carefully turn on a wire rack to cool completely before serving.

Serve with the sprinkling of brown sugar.

NUTTY CRANBERRY MUFFINS

Time: 25 minutes   Servings: 12

Ingredients:

1¼ cups all-purpose flour   1 egg
½ teaspoon baking soda   ½ teaspoon vanilla essence
½ teaspoon baking powder   ¾ cup milk
½ cup granulated sugar   ½ cup fresh cranberries
1/3 cup salted butter, softened   ½ cup walnuts, chopped

Directions:

In a bowl, sift together flour, baking soda and baking powder.

In another bowl, add sugar and butter and beat till creamy

Add egg and vanilla extract and beat till well combined.

Add flour mixture alternately with milk into egg mixture and mix till just combined.

Fold in cranberries and walnuts.

Preheat the Airfryer to 320 degrees F.

Grease 12 muffin molds.

Transfer the mixture into prepared muffin molds evenly.

Cook for about 10 minutes or till a toothpick inserted in the center comes out clean.

Remove the muffin molds from Airfryer and keep on wire rack to cool for about 15 minutes.

Carefully turn on a wire rack to cool completely before serving.

SPICED CHERRY MUFFINS

Time: 25 minutes   Servings: 4

Ingredients:

1/3 cup flour   ½ teaspoon baking powder
3 tablespoons granulated sugar   ½ teaspoon ground cinnamon
½ teaspoon baking soda   ½ teaspoon ground nutmeg

Pinch of ground cloves

Pinch of salt

1 egg

½ cup unsalted butter, melted

1/3 cup milk

1/3 cup dried cherries

Directions:

In a bowl, mix together flour, sugar, baking soda, baking powder, spices and salt.

In another bowl, add egg, butter and milk and beat till well combined.

Add flour mixture into egg mixture and mix till just combined.

Fold in cherries.

Preheat the Airfryer at 390 degrees F.

Grease 4 doubled muffin molds.

Transfer the mixture into prepared muffin molds evenly.

Cook for about 15 minutes or till a toothpick inserted in the center comes out clean.

Remove the muffin molds from Airfryer and keep on wire rack to cool for about 15 minutes.

Carefully turn on a wire rack to cool completely before serving.

OAT & RAISINS MUFFINS

Time: 20 minutes

Servings: 4

Ingredients:

½ cup flour

¼ cup rolled oats

1/8 teaspoon baking powder

½ cup powdered sugar

½ cup butter, softened

2 eggs

¼ teaspoon vanilla extract

¼ cup raisins

Directions:

In a bowl, mix together flour, oats and baking powder.

In another bowl, add sugar and butter and beat till creamy

Add egg and vanilla extract and beat till well combined.

Add egg mixture into oat mixture and mix till just combined.

Fold in raisins.

Preheat the Airfryer to 355 degrees F.

Grease 4 muffin molds.

Transfer the mixture into prepared muffin molds evenly.

Cook for about 10 minutes or till a toothpick inserted in the center comes out clean.

Remove the muffin molds from Airfryer and keep on wire rack to cool for about 10 minutes.

Carefully turn on a wire rack to cool completely before serving.

OAT &PUMPKIN MUFFINS

Time: 25 minutes

Servings: 12

Ingredients:

2 cups oats

1 cup pumpkin puree

½ cup honey

2 medium eggs, beaten

1 tablespoon cacao nibs

1 teaspoon coconut butter

1 tablespoon vanilla essence

1 teaspoon ground nutmeg

Directions:

In a blender, add all ingredients and pulse till smooth.

Preheat the Airfryer to 355 degrees F.

Grease 12 muffin molds.

Transfer the mixture into prepared muffin molds evenly.

Cook for about 15 minutes or till a toothpick inserted in the center comes out clean.

Remove the muffin molds from Airfryer and keep on wire rack to cool for about 10 minutes.

Carefully turn on a wire rack to cool completely before serving.

OAT & BANANA MUFFINS

Time: 25 minutes   Servings: 4

Ingredients:

¼ cup oats

¼ cup refined flour

½ teaspoon baking powder

¼ cup powdered sugar

¼ cup unsalted butter, softened

¼ cup banana, peeled and mashed

1 teaspoon milk

1 tablespoon pecans, chopped

Directions:

In a bowl, mix together oats, flour and baking powder.

In another bowl, add sugar and butter and beat till creamy

Add banana and vanilla extract and beat till well combined.

Add flour mixture and milk in banana mixture and mix till just combined.

Fold in pecans.

Preheat the Airfryer to 320 degrees F.

Grease 4 muffin molds.

Transfer the mixture into prepared muffin molds evenly.

Cook for about 10 minutes or till a toothpick inserted in the center comes out clean.

Remove the muffin molds from Airfryer and keep on wire rack to cool for about 15 minutes.

Carefully turn on a wire rack to cool completely before serving.

CHOCOLATE MUFFINS

Time: 25 minutes   Servings: 12

Ingredients:

1 1/3 cups self-rising flour

2/3 cup plus 3 tablespoons caster sugar

2 ½ tablespoons cocoa powder

3½-ounce butter

5 tablespoons milk

2 medium eggs

½ teaspoon vanilla extract

Water, as required

2½-ounce milk chocolate, chopped finely

Directions:

In a bowl, mix together flour, sugar and cocoa powder.

With a pastry cutter, cut the butter till a breadcrumb like mixture forms.

In another bowl, add milk and egg and beat well.

Add egg mixture in flour mixture and mix till well combined.

Add vanilla extract and a little water and mix till well combined.

Fold in chopped chocolate.

Preheat the Airfryer to 355 degrees F.

Grease 4 muffin molds.

Transfer the mixture into prepared muffin molds evenly.

Cook for about 9 minutes.

Now, set the Airfryer to 320 degrees F.

Cook for about 6 minutes or till a toothpick inserted in the center comes out clean.

Remove the muffin molds from Airfryer and keep on wire rack to cool for about 15 minutes.

Carefully turn on a wire rack to cool completely before serving.

CHOCOLATY BANANA MUFFINS

Time: 35 minutes   Servings: 12

Ingredients:

¾ cup whole wheat flour
¾ cup plain flour
¼ cup cocoa powder
¼ teaspoon baking powder
1 teaspoon baking soda
¼ teaspoon salt

2 large bananas, peeled and mashed
1 cup sugar
1/3 cup canola oil
1 egg
½ teaspoon vanilla essence
1 cup mini chocolate chips

Directions:

In a large bowl, mix together flour, cocoa powder, baking powder, baking soda and salt.

In another bowl, add bananas, sugar, oil, egg and vanilla extract and beat till well combined.

Slowly, add flour mixture in egg mixture and mix till just combined.

Fold in chocolate chips.

Preheat the Airfryer to 345 degrees F.

Grease 12 muffin molds.

Transfer the mixture into prepared muffin molds evenly.

Cook for about 20-25 minutes or till a toothpick inserted in the center comes out clean.

Remove the muffin molds from Airfryer and keep on wire rack to cool for about 10 minutes.

Carefully turn on a wire rack to cool completely before serving.

Chocolaty & Nutty Yogurt Muffins

Time: 20 minutes   Servings: 9

Ingredients:

1½ cups all-purpose flour   1/3 cup vegetable oil
¼ cup sugar   1 egg
2 teaspoons baking powder   2 teaspoons vanilla extract
½ teaspoon salt   ¼ cup mini chocolate chips
1 cup yogurt   ¼ cup pecans, chopped

Directions:

In a large bowl, mix together flour, sugar, baking powder and salt.

In another bowl, add yogurt, oil, egg and vanilla extract and beat till well combined.

Add flour mixture in egg mixture and mix till just combined.

Fold in chocolate chips and pecans.

Preheat the Airfryer to 355 degrees F.

Grease 9 muffin molds.

Transfer the mixture into prepared muffin molds evenly.

Cook for about 10 minutes or till a toothpick inserted in the center comes out clean.

Remove the muffin molds from Airfryer and keep on wire rack to cool for about 10 minutes.

Carefully turn on a wire rack to cool completely before serving.

Fudge Brownies Muffins

Time: 20 minutes   Servings: 12

Ingredients:

1 package Betty Crocker fudge brownie mix   1/3 cup vegetable oil
¼ cup walnuts, chopped   2 teaspoon water
1 egg

Directions:

Preheat the Airfryer to 300 degrees F.

Grease 12 muffin molds.

In a bowl, add all ingredients and mix till well combined.

Transfer the mixture into prepared muffin molds evenly.

Cook for about 10 minutes or till a toothpick inserted in the center comes out clean.

Remove the muffin molds from Airfryer and keep on wire rack to cool for about 10 minutes.

Carefully turn on a wire rack to cool completely before serving.

BLUEBERRY & YOGURT MUFFINS

Time: 20 minutes   Servings: 10

Ingredients:

1½ cups cake flour   1/3 cup vegetable oil
½ cup sugar   1 egg
2 teaspoons baking powder   2 teaspoons vanilla extract
½ teaspoon salt   1 cup fresh blueberries
1 cup yogurt

Directions:

In a large bowl, mix together flour, sugar, baking powder and salt.

In another bowl, add yogurt, oil, egg and vanilla extract and beat till well combined.

Add flour mixture in egg mixture and mix till just combined.

Fold in chocolate chips. Preheat the Airfryer to 355 degrees F.

Grease 10 muffin molds.

Transfer the mixture into prepared muffin molds evenly.

Cook for about 10 minutes or till a toothpick inserted in the center comes out clean.

Remove the muffin molds from Airfryer and keep on wire rack to cool for about 10 minutes.

Carefully turn on a wire rack to cool completely before serving.

SPICED APPLE & YOGURT MUFFINS

Time: 20 minutes   Servings: 10

Ingredients:

1½ cups cake flour   ½ teaspoon salt
½ cup white sugar   1 cup yogurt
2 teaspoons baking powder   1/3 cup olive oil
½ teaspoon ground cinnamon   1 egg
¼ teaspoon ground ginger   1½ teaspoons vanilla extract
¼ teaspoon ground cloves   1 cup apple, peeled, cored and chopped

Directions:

In a large bowl, mix together flour, sugar, baking powder and salt.

In another bowl, add yogurt, oil, egg and vanilla extract and beat till well combined.

Add flour mixture in egg mixture and mix till just combined.

Fold in chocolate chips.

Preheat the Airfryer to 355 degrees F.

Grease 10 muffin molds.

Transfer the mixture into prepared muffin molds evenly.

Cook for about 10 minutes or till a toothpick inserted in the center comes out clean.

Remove the muffin molds from Airfryer and keep on wire rack to cool for about 10 minutes.

Carefully turn on a wire rack to cool completely before serving.

Nutty Milk Tea Muffins

Time: 20 minutes   Servings: 7

Ingredients:

5 tablespoons milk
2 (3-in-1) sachet instant milk tea powder
3 tablespoons sugar
1 egg
¼ cup olive oil

½ teaspoon vanilla extract
½ cup cake flour
1 teaspoon baking powder
½ cup walnuts

Directions:

Preheat the Airfryer to 248 degrees F.
Ina baking dish, add milk and heat in Airfryer for about 5 minutes.
Remove from Airfryer and stir in tea milk powder and keep aside.
In a bowl, add sugar and egg and beat till fluffy.
Add oil and vanilla extract and mix till well combined.
In another bowl, mix together flour, baking powder and walnuts.
Make a well in the center of flour mixture.
Add milk mixture and egg mixture into flour mixture and mix till just combined.
Preheat the Airfryer to 300 degrees F.
Grease 10 muffin molds.
Transfer the mixture into prepared muffin molds evenly.
Cook for about 10 minutes or till a toothpick inserted in the center comes out clean.
Remove the muffin molds from Airfryer and keep on wire rack to cool for about 10 minutes.
Carefully turn on a wire rack to cool completely before serving.

Savory Carrot Muffins

Time: 25 minutes   Servings: 6

Ingredients:

For Muffins:

¼ cup whole wheat flour
¼ cup all-purpose flour
1/8 teaspoon baking soda
½ teaspoon baking powder
½ teaspoon dried parsley, crushed
½ teaspoon salt
½ cup yogurt

1 teaspoon vinegar
1 tablespoon vegetable oil
3 tablespoons cottage cheese, grated
1 carrot, peeled and grated
2-4 tablespoons water (if required)

For the Toping:
7-ounce parmesan cheese, grated
¼ cup walnuts, chopped

Directions:

For muffins in a large bowl, mix together flours, baking soda, baking powder, parsley and salt
In another large bowl, add yogurt and vinegar and beat well.

Add remaining ingredients except water and beat well.

(add required amount of water if required)

Make a well in the center of yogurt mixture.

Slowly, add flour mixture in the well and mix till well combined.

Preheat the Airfryer to 355 degrees F.

Grease 6 muffin molds.

Transfer the mixture into the prepared muffin molds evenly.

Top with Parmesan and walnuts.

Place the muffin molds in a fryer basket in 2 batches.

Bake for about 7 minutes or till a tooth pick inserted in the center comes out clean.

Remove the muffin molds from Airfryer and keep on wire rack to cool for about 10 minutes.

Carefully turn on a wire rack to cool completely before serving.

Cheesy Muffins

Time: 20 minutes   Servings: 8

Ingredients:
2/3 cup plain flour   ¼ cup milk
1 teaspoon baking powder   2 tablespoons canola oil
Pinch of mustard powder   ¼ cup Parmesan cheese, grated
1 small egg   Dash of Worcestershire sauce

Directions:
In a large bowl, mix together flour, baking powder and mustard powder.

In another bowl, add egg and milk and beat till well combined.

Add egg mixture into flour mixture and mix till well combined.

Stir in cheese and Worcestershire sauce.

Preheat the Airfryer to 390 degrees F.

Grease 8 muffin molds.

Transfer the mixture into the prepared muffin molds evenly.

Bake for about 15 minutes or till a tooth pick inserted in the center comes out clean.

Remove the muffin molds from Airfryer and keep on wire rack to cool for about 10 minutes.

Carefully turn on a wire rack to cool completely before serving.

Lunch Recipes

BREADED CHICKEN

Time: 25 minutes   Servings: 4

Ingredients:
1 egg, beaten   ½ cup breadcrumbs
2 tablespoons vegetable oil   8 skinless, boneless chicken tenderloins

Directions:
In a shallow dish, beat the egg.
In another shallow dish, add oil and breadcrumbs and mix till a crumbly mixture forms.
Dip the chicken tenderloins in egg evenly and then coat in the breadcrumbs mixture.
Shake off the excess coating.
Preheat the air fryer to 355 degrees F.
Place the chicken tenderloins in the Airfryer.
Cook for about 12 minutes

SWEET & SOUR CHICKEN WINGS

Time: 20 minutes   Servings: 2

Ingredients:

For Wings Marinade: **For Sprinkling:**

1 teaspoon garlic, chopped finely   2 tablespoons all-purpose flour
1 tablespoon fresh lemon juice
1 tablespoon soy sauce   **For Sauce:**
½ teaspoon dried oregano, crushed   2 teaspoons scallions, chopped finely
Salt and freshly ground black pepper, to   1 teaspoon brown sugar
taste   1 tablespoon tomato ketchup
8 chicken wings   1 tablespoon vinegar
                                        1 tablespoon chili sauce

Directions:
For marinade in a large bowl, mix together all ingredients except wings.
Add wings and coat with marinade generously.
Refrigerate, covered for about 2 hour.
Preheat the air fryer to 355 degrees F.
Remove the chicken wings from marinade and sprinkle with flour evenly.
Place the wing in an Airfryer tray.
Cook for about 6 minutes, flipping once after 3 minutes
Meanwhile in a bowl, add all sauce ingredients and mix till well combined.

Remove chicken wings from Air fryer tray and coat with sauce generously.
Return the wings in Airfryer and cook for about 2-3 minutes more.
Serve hot.

*B*UFFALO CHICKEN WINGS

Time: 25 minutes   Servings: 2

Ingredients:

6 chicken wings
2 teaspoons cayenne pepper
½ teaspoon garlic powder

Salt and freshly ground black pepper to taste
1 tablespoon butter, melted
2 tablespoons red hot sauce

Directions:

Preheat the air fryer to 355 degrees F.
Cut the wings into 3 portions at the joint. With paper towel, pat dry the wings.
In a shallow dish, mix together cayenne pepper, garlic powder, salt and black pepper.
Lightly coat the chicken wings with the spice mixture.
Arrange chicken wings onto a wire rack in Airfryer in a single layer.
Cook for about 15 minutes, turning once in the middle.
In a bowl, mix together melted butter, hot sauce, salt and pepper.
Coat the chicken wings with sauce before serving.

*B*READED CHICKEN WINGS

Time: 40 minutes   Servings: 2

Ingredients:

2 stalk of lemongrass (white portion), minced
1 onion, chopped finely
1 tablespoon soy sauce
1½ tablespoons honey

Salt and freshly ground white pepper, to taste
8 chicken wings, rinsed and trimmed
Potato starch, as required

Directions:

In a bowl, mix together all ingredients except wings and potato starch.
Add wings and coat with marinade generously.
Cover and refrigerate to marinate for overnight.
Preheat the air fryer to 355 degrees F.
Remove the chicken wings from marinade.
Coat the chicken wings with potato starch.
Arrange the chicken wings in Airfryer basket.
Cook for about 15 minutes.
Flip the side and cook for about10 minutes.

ZINGY & NUTTY CHICKEN WINGS

Time: 20 minutes

Servings: 4

Ingredients:

1 tablespoon fish sauce
1 tablespoon fresh lemon juice
1 teaspoon sugar

12 chicken middle wings, cut into half
2 fresh lemongrass stalks, chopped finely
¼ cup unsalted cashews, crushed

Directions:

In a bowl, mix together fish sauce, lime juice and sugar.

Add wings ad coat with mixture generously.

Refrigerate to marinate for about 1-2 hours.

Preheat the air fryer to 355 degrees F.

In an Airfryer pan, place lemongrass stalks.

Cook for about 2-3 minutes.

Remove the cashew mixture from Airfryer and transfer into a bowl.

Now, set the Airfryer to 390 degrees F.

Place the chicken wings in Airfryer pan.

Cook for about 13-15 minutes further.

Transfer the wings into serving plates.

Sprinkle with cashew mixture and serve.

CHICKEN WINGS WITH PRAWN PASTE

Time: 20 minutes

Servings: 3

Ingredients:

2 tablespoons olive plus extra for coating
1 tablespoon prawn paste
¾ teaspoon sugar
1 teaspoon sesame oil

1 teaspoon fresh ginger juice
½ teaspoon Shaoxing wine
1 pound mid-joint chicken wings
Corn flour, as required

Directions:

In a bowl, mix together all ingredients except wings and corn flour.

Add chicken wings and coat with marinade generously.

Refrigerate for overnight.

Just before cooking, coat the chicken wings with corn flour evenly.

Shake off the excess flour.

Preheat the air fryer to 355 degrees F.

Coat the wings with a little extra oil.

Arrange the chicken wings in Airfryer basket.

Cook for about 8 minutes.

BREADED CHICKEN TENDERLOINS

Time: 30 minutes   Servings: 4

Ingredients:

1 egg, beaten   1 cup breadcrumbs
2 tablespoon vegetable oil   8 chicken tenderloins

Directions:

Preheat the air fryer to 355 degrees F.
In a bowl, beat the egg.
In another bowl, add oil and breadcrumbs and mix till the mixture becomes crumbly.
Dip the chicken into the egg and then coat with the crumb mixture evenly.
Arrange the chicken tenderloins in Airfryer basket.
Cook for about 12 minutes.

CRUSTED CHICKEN TENDERS

Time: 25 minutes   Servings: 3

Ingredients:

½ cup all-purpose flour   Salt and freshly ground black pepper, to
2 eggs, beaten   taste
½ cup seasoned breadcrumbs   2 tablespoons olive oil
                                                    ¾ pound chicken tenders

Directions:

In a bowl, place the flour
In a second bowl, place the eggs.
In a third bowl, mix together breadcrumbs, salt, black pepper and oil.
Coat the chicken tenders in the flour,
Then dip into the eggs and finally coat with the breadcrumbs mixture evenly.
Preheat the air fryer to 330 degrees F.
Arrange the chicken tenderloins in Airfryer basket.
Cook for about 10 minutes.
Now, set the Airfryer to 390 degrees F.
Cook for about 5 minutes further.

GLAZED CHICKEN TENDERS

Time: 15 minutes   Servings: 2

Ingredients:

2 cups ketchup   2 tablespoons honey
1 cup brown sugar   2 skinless, boneless chicken tenders

Directions:

Preheat the air fryer to 355 degrees F.

In a bowl, mix together all ingredients except chicken tenders.

Add chicken tenders and coat with glaze generously.

Arrange the chicken tenderloins in Airfryer basket.

Cook for about 8 minutes.

Spice & Herbs Crusted Chicken

Time: 30 minutes   Servings: 2

Ingredients:

1 cup plain flour
3 eggs, beaten
3 cups breadcrumbs
3 teaspoons oregano
3 teaspoons parsley
2 teaspoons thyme

2 teaspoons paprika
1 teaspoon cayenne pepper
Salt and freshly ground black pepper, to taste
½ pound chicken pieces

Directions:

Preheat the air fryer to 350 degrees F.

In a bowl, place the flour

In a second bowl, place the eggs.

In a third bowl, mix together remaining ingredients except chicken pieces.

Coat the chicken tenders in the flour,

Then dip into the eggs and finally coat with the breadcrumbs mixture evenly.

Arrange the chicken pieces in Airfryer basket.

Cook for about 18 minutes.

Buttered Scallops

Time: 15 minutes   Servings: 2

Ingredients:

¾ pound sea scallops
1 tablespoon butter, melted
½ tablespoon fresh thyme, minced

Salt and freshly ground black pepper, to taste

Directions:

Preheat the Airfryer to 390 degrees F.

In a large bowl, add all ingredients and toss to coat well.

Arrange the scallops in an Airfryer basket.

Cook for about 4 minutes.

HAM WRAPPED PRAWNS

Time: 30 minutes

Servings: 4

Ingredients:

1 large red bell pepper
1 garlic clove, minced
1 tablespoon olive oil
½ tablespoon paprika

Salt and freshly ground black pepper, to taste
8 king prawns, peeled and deveined
4 ham slices, halved

Directions:

Preheat the air fryer to 425 degrees F.
Place the bell pepper in a fryer basket
Cook for about 10 minutes.
Transfer the bell pepper into a bowl and immediately cover with a foil paper.
Keep aside for about 15 minutes.
Peel the pepper and remove the seeds and stems, then chop it.
In a blender, add chopped bell pepper, garlic, paprika and oil and pulse till a puree forms.
Keep aside.
Wrap each prawn with a slice of ham.
Grease the fryer basket and arrange the prawns in it.
Cook for about 3 minutes till golden browned.
Serve the prawns with bell pepper dip.

NACHO CHIPS CRUSTED PRAWNS

Time: 20 minutes

Servings: 5

Ingredients:

18-20 prawns, peeled and deveined
1 large egg
10-ounce Nacho flavored chips, crushed finely

Directions:

In a bowl, beat the egg.
In another bowl, place the nacho chips
Dip each prawn into the beaten egg and then coat with the crushed nacho chips.
Preheat the air fryer to 350 degrees F.
Place the prawns in the Airfryer.
Cook for about 8 minutes.

BREADED SHRIMP WITH SAUCE

Time: 45 minutes   Servings: 4

Ingredients:

For Shrimp:

8 large shrimp, peeled and deveined
Salt and freshly ground black pepper, to taste
8 ounces coconut milk
½ cup panko breadcrumbs

½ teaspoon cayenne pepper

For Sauce:

½ cup orange marmalade
1 teaspoon mustard
¼ teaspoon hot sauce
1 tablespoon honey

Directions:

Preheat the air fryer to 350 degrees F.

In a shallow dish, mix together salt, black pepper and coconut milk.

In another shallow dish, mix together breadcrumbs, cayenne pepper, salt and black pepper.

Coat the shrimp in coconut milk mixture and then roll into breadcrumbs mixture.

Place the shrimp in the Airfryer.

Cook for about 20 minutes or till desired doneness.

Meanwhile for sauce in a bowl mix together all sauce ingredients.

Serve shrimp with sauce.

SPICY SHRIMP

Time: 15 minutes   Servings: 2

Ingredients:

½ pound tiger shrimp
1 tablespoon olive oil
½ teaspoon old bay seasoning

¼ teaspoon smoked paprika
¼ teaspoon cayenne pepper
Salt, to taste

Directions:

Preheat the Airfryer to 390 degrees F.

In a large bowl, add all ingredients and mix till well combined.

Place the shrimp in an Airfryer basket.

Cook for about 5 minutes.

BACON WRAPPED SHRIMP

Time: 25 minutes   Servings: 4

Ingredients:

1¼ pound tiger shrimp, peeled and deveined
1 pound bacon

Directions:

Wrap each shrimp with a slice of bacon.

Refrigerate for about 20 minutes.

Preheat the Airfryer to 390 degrees F.

Arrange the shrimp in Airfryer basket.

Cook for about 5-7 minutes.

Coconut Crusted Shrimp

Time: 35 minutes   Servings: 2-3

Ingredients:

8 large shrimp, peeled and deveined

8-ounce coconut milk

Salt and freshly ground black pepper, to taste

½ cup sweetened coconut, shredded

½ cup panko breadcrumbs

½ cup orange marmalade

1 tablespoon honey

1 teaspoon mustard

¼ teaspoon hot sauce

Directions:

In a small bowl, add coconut milk, salt and black pepper and beat till well combined. Keep aside.

In another small bowl, mix together coconut, panko, salt and pepper.

Dip the shrimp in the coconut milk mixture and then coat with the panko mixture.

Preheat the air fryer to 350 degrees F.

Place the shrimp in Airfryer basket.

Cook for about 20 minutes.

Meanwhile in a bowl, add the marmalade, honey, mustard and hot sauce and beat till well combined.

Serve the shrimp with the sauce.

Lemony & Spicy Coconut Crusted Shrimp

Time: 15 minutes   Servings: 4

Ingredients:

1 pound large shrimp, peeled and de-veined

½ cup flour

2 egg whites

½ cup breadcrumbs

½ cup unsweetened coconut, shredded

¼ teaspoon lemon zest

Salt and freshly ground black pepper, to taste

¼ teaspoon cayenne pepper

¼ teaspoon red pepper flakes, crushed

Vegetable oil, as required

Directions:

In a shallow dish, mix together the flour, salt and pepper.

In a second shallow dish, beat the eggs.

In a third shallow dish, mix together the breadcrumbs, coconut, lime zest, salt and cayenne pepper.

Preheat the Airfryer to 400 degrees F.

Coat each shrimp in the flour, then dip in the egg and then into the breadcrumb evenly.

Place the shrimp in the Airfryer basket and drizzle with vegetable oil.

Cook for about 5-6 minutes.

*L*EMONY TUNA

Time: 30 minutes   Servings: 4

Ingredients:
2 (6-ounce) cans water packed plain tuna
2 teaspoons Dijon mustard
½ cup breadcrumbs
1 tablespoon fresh lime juice
2 tablespoons fresh parsley, chopped

1 egg
Dash of hot sauce
3 tablespoons canola oil
Salt and freshly ground black pepper, to taste

Directions:
Drain most of the liquid from the canned tuna.

In a bowl, add the fish, mustard, crumbs, citrus juice, parsley and hot sauce and mix till well combined.

Add a little canola oil if it seems too dry.

Add egg, salt and stir to combine.

Make the patties from tuna mixture.

Refrigerate the tuna patties for about 2 hours.

Preheat the air fryer to 355 degrees F.

Cook for about 10-12 minutes.

*T*UNA STUFFED POTATOES

Time: 45 minutes   Servings: 4

Ingredients:
4 starchy potatoes
½ tablespoon olive oil
1 (6-ounce) can tuna, drained
2 tablespoons plain Greek yogurt
1 teaspoon red chili powder

Salt and freshly ground black pepper, to taste
1 scallion, chopped and divided
1 tablespoon capers

Directions:
In a large bowl of water, soak the potatoes for about 30 minutes.

Drain well and pat dry with paper towel.

Preheat the air fryer to 355 degrees F.

Place the potatoes in a fryer basket.

Cook for about 30 minutes.

Meanwhile in a bowl, add tuna, yogurt, red chili powder, salt, black pepper and half of scallion and with a potato masher, mash the mixture completely.

Remove the potatoes from the Airfryer and place onto a smooth surface.

Carefully, cut each potato from top side lengthwise.
With your fingers, press the open side of potato halves slightly.
Stuff the potato open portion with tuna mixture evenly.
Sprinkle with the capers and remaining scallion.
Serve immediately.

ADISH SALAD

Time: 45 minutes   Servings: 4

Ingredients:

For Radishes:

1½ pounds radishes, trimmed and halved
Salt and freshly ground black pepper, to taste
2 tablespoons olive oil

For the Salad:

½ pound fresh mozzarella, sliced
1 teaspoon honey
1 teaspoon olive oil
1 tablespoon balsamic vinegar
Salt and freshly ground black pepper, to taste

Directions:

In a large bowl, add radishes, salt, black pepper and oil and toss to coat well.
Preheat the air fryer to 350 degrees F.
Place the radishes in a fryer basket
Cook for about 30 minutes, tossing 2-3 times.
For salad in a serving bowl, mix together the cooked radishes and cheese.
In a small bowl, mix together remaining ingredients.
Drizzle vinaigrette over salad and toss to coat.

*H*ONEY GLAZED CARROTS

Time: 25 minutes   Servings: 4

Ingredients:

3 cups carrots, peeled and cut into large chunks
1 tablespoon olive oil

1 tablespoon honey
Salt and freshly ground black pepper, to taste

Directions:

Preheat the Airfryer to 390 degrees F.
In a bowl, add all ingredients and toss to coat well.
Place the carrots in Airfryer.
Cook for about 12 minutes.

CARAMELIZED CARROTS

Time: 25 minutes   Servings: 3

Ingredients:
½ cup butter, melted   1 small bag baby carrots
½ cup brown sugar

Directions:
Preheat the Airfryer to 400 degrees F.
In a bowl, mix together butter and brown sugar.
Add carrots and sugar and coat well.
Cook for about 15 minutes.

CARROTS WITH ZUCCHINI

Time: 50 minutes   Servings: 4

Ingredients:
½ pound carrots peeled and cut into 1-inch   2 pound zucchini, trimmed and cut into
cubes   ¾-inch half moons
6 teaspoons olive oil   Salt and freshly ground white pepper, to
                                               taste

Directions:
Preheat the Airfryer to 400 degrees F.
In a small bowl, add the carrot cubes, 2 teaspoons of the oil and toss to coat.
Place the carrots in an Airfryer basket. Cook for about 5 minutes.
Meanwhile in a bowl, add the zucchini, remaining 4 teaspoons of oil, salt and pepper and toss to coat.
After 5 minutes, place the zucchini in the basket.
Cook for about 30 minutes, tossing 3 times.
Serve warm.

SPICY EGGPLANTS

Time: 25 minutes   Servings: 6

Ingredients:
3 eggplants, halved   Salt and freshly ground black pepper, to
2 tablespoons olive oil   taste

Directions:
Preheat the Airfryer to 400 degrees F.
Coat the eggplant halves with oil generously and sprinkle with salt and pepper.
Place the eggplants in Airfryer basket.
Cook for about 12-15 minutes.

$\mathcal{T}$OMATOES WITH BASIL

Time: 20 minutes   Servings: 2

Ingredients:

2 tomatoes, halved   Freshly ground black pepper, to taste
Cooking spray, as required   1 tablespoon fresh basil, chopped

Directions:

Preheat the Airfryer to 320 degrees F.
Drizzle cut sides of the tomato halves with cooking spray evenly.
Sprinkle with black pepper and basil.
In an Airfryer tray, arrange the tomato halves, cut sides up.
Cook for about 10 minutes or till desired doneness.

$\mathcal{H}$EIRLOOM TOMATOES WITH PESTO

Time: 35 minutes   Servings: 4

Ingredients:

For Pesto: **For Tomatoes:**

½ cup plus 1 tablespoon olive oil, divided 2 heirloom tomatoes, cut into ½ inch thick
3 tablespoons pine nuts   slices.
Salt, to taste   8-ounce feta cheese, cut into ½ inch thick
½ cup fresh basil, chopped   slices.
½ cup fresh parsley, chopped   ½ cup red onions, sliced thinly
1 garlic clove, chopped   1 tablespoon olive oil
½ cup Parmesan cheese, grated   Salt, to taste

Directions:

Preheat the Airfryer to 390 degrees F.
In a bowl, add 1 tablespoon of oil, pine nuts and pinch of salt
Place the pine nuts in Airfryer and cook for about 1-2 minutes.
Transfer the pine nuts onto a paper towel lined plate.
In a food processor, add toasted pine nuts, fresh herbs, garlic, Parmesan and salt and pulse till just combined.
While motor is running, slowly add oil and pulse till smooth.
Transfer into a bowl and refrigerate, covered till serving.
Spread the 1 tablespoon pesto on each slice of tomato.
Top with a feta slice and onion and drizzle with oil.
Place the prepared tomato slices into Airfryer.
Cook for about 12-14 minutes.
Serve with remaining pesto.

BACON WRAPPED ASPARAGUS

Time: 30 minutes   Servings: 4

Ingredients:

1 garlic clove, minced   1 pound asparagus
1½ tablespoons brown sugar   4 bacon slices
1½ tablespoons olive oil   ½ tablespoon toasted sesame seeds
½ tablespoon sesame oil, toasted

Directions:

Preheat the air fryer to 355 degrees F.

In a bowl, add the garlic, brown sugar and both oils and mix till the sugar dissolves.

Divide the asparagus into four equal bunches and wrap each bunch with a bacon slice.

Coat each asparagus bunch with oil mixture.

Arrange the asparagus bunches in an Airfryer basket.

Sprinkle with sesame seeds evenly.

Cook for about 8 minutes.

SPICY POTATOES

Time: 30 minutes   Servings: 4

Ingredients:

1¾ pound waxy potatoes, peeled and   1 tablespoon paprika, divided
cubed   Salt and freshly ground black pepper
2 tablespoons olive oil, divided   ½ cup Greek plain yogurt

Directions:

In a large bowl of water, add the potatoes and keep aside for about 30 minutes.

Drain completely and dry with paper towels.

Transfer the potatoes into a large bowl.

Add 1 tablespoon olive oil, paprika and black pepper and toss to coat well.

Preheat the air fryer to 355 degrees F.

Place the potatoes into the fryer basket.

Cook for about 20 minutes or till potatoes become golden brown.

In a small bowl, mix together yogurt, remaining oil, salt and pepper.

In a serving plate, place the potatoes and serve alongside the yogurt as a dip.

GARLICKY POTATOES

Time: 1 hour   Servings: 4

Ingredients:

3 Russel potatoes   1-2 tablespoons olive oil

1 tablespoon garlic, minced

Salt, to taste

1 teaspoon dried parsley flakes, crushed

Directions:

Preheat the Airfryer to 390 degrees F.

With a fork, prick the potatoes.

Drizzle with the oil and rub with garlic, parsley and salt.

Arrange the potatoes in an Airfryer basket.

Cook for about 35-40 minutes.

JACKET POTATOES

Time: 25 minutes

Servings: 2

Ingredients:

2 potatoes

1 teaspoon chives, minced

1 tablespoon mozzarella cheese, shredded

Salt and freshly ground black pepper, to

3 tablespoons sour cream

taste

1 tablespoon butter, softened

Directions:

Preheat the Airfryer to 355 degrees F.

With a fork, prick the potatoes.

Place the potatoes in Airfryer basket.

Cook for about for about 15 minutes.

In a bowl, add remaining ingredients and mix till well combined.

Open the potatoes in the centre and stuff them with the cheese mixture.

Serve immediately

CHEESE STUFFED POTATOES

Time: 50 minutes

Servings: 4

Ingredients:

4 potatoes, peeled

½ of brown onion, chopped

Oil, as required

½ cup Parmesan cheese, grated

2 bacon rashers

Directions:

Preheat the Airfryer to 390 degrees F.

Coat the potatoes with the oil.

Place the potatoes in Airfryer basket.

Cook for about for about 10 minutes, coating with the oil twice.

After 10 minutes coat the potatoes with oil again.

Remove from the Airfryer and cut each potato in half.

Scoop out the flesh from each half.

Heat a frying pan on medium heat and cook the bacon and onion for about 5-6 minutes.

Transfer the bacon mixture into a bowl.

Add half of the cheese and stir to combine.

Stuff the potato halves with potato mixture evenly.

Sprinkle with remaining cheese.

Cook the potatoes in the Airfryer for about 6 minutes.

SWEET & SPICY PARSNIPS

Time: 55 minutes   Servings: 6

Ingredients:

2 pound parsnip, peeled and cut into 1-inch chunks

1 tablespoon butter, melted

2 tablespoons maple syrup

1 tablespoon dried parsley flakes, crushed

¼ teaspoon red pepper flakes, crushed

Directions:

Preheat the air fryer to 355 degrees F.

In a large bowl, add parsnips and duck fat and toss to coat well.

Transfer the parsnip in an Airfryer basket and cook for about 40 minutes.

Meanwhile in a large bowl, mix together remaining ingredients.

After 40 minutes, transfer the parsnips into the bowl with maple syrup mixture and toss to coat well.

Cook for about 3-4 minutes more.

LEMONY BRUSSELS SPROUT

Time: 45 minutes   Servings: 3

Ingredients:

1 pound fresh medium Brussels sprouts, trimmed and halved vertically

1 tablespoon fresh lemon juice

3 teaspoons olive oil

Salt and freshly ground black pepper, to taste

Directions:

Preheat the Airfryer to 400 degrees F. In a bowl, add all ingredients and toss to coat well.

Spread the Brussels sprouts onto a large baking sheet.

Cook for about25-35 minutes

BUTTERED BRUSSELS SPROUT

Time: 45 minutes   Servings: 4

Ingredients:

1 pound Brussels sprouts, trimmed and halved

Salt and freshly ground black pepper, to taste

4 teaspoons butter, melted

Directions:

Preheat the Airfryer to 400 degrees F.

In a large bowl, add all ingredients and toss to coat well.

Place the Brussels sprouts in an Airfryer basket.

Cook for about 25-35 minutes.

LEMONY BROCCOLI

Time: 50 minutes   Servings: 4

Ingredients:

1 tablespoon butter

2 teaspoons chicken bouillon granules

1 tablespoon fresh lemon juice

3 garlic cloves, chopped

1 large head broccoli, cut into bite-sized pieces

1 tablespoon white sesame seeds

½ teaspoon fresh lemon zest, grated finely

½ teaspoon red pepper flakes, crushed

Directions:

Preheat the air fryer to 355 degrees F.

In an Airfryer pan, mix together the butter, chicken bouillon granules and lemon juice and cook for about 2 minutes.

Stir in garlic and cook for about 30 seconds.

Add broccoli and cook for about 13 minutes.

Add sesame seeds, lemon zest and red pepper flakes and cook for 5 minutes.

CHEESY BROCCOLI & OLIVES

Time: 25 minutes   Servings: 2

Ingredients:

2 pound broccoli, stemmed and cut into 1 inch florets

2 tablespoons olive oil

Salt and freshly ground black pepper, to taste

1/3 cup Kalamata olives, halved and pitted

2 teaspoons fresh lemon zest, grated

¼ cup Parmesan cheese, grated

Directions:

In a pan of boiling water, add broccoli and cook for about 3-4 minutes.

Drain well.

Preheat the Airfryer to 400 degrees F.

In a bowl, add broccoli, oil, salt and pepper and toss to coat.

Place broccoli in an Airfryer basket.

Cook for about 15 minutes, tossing once in the middle way.

Remove from the oven and immediately stir in the olives, lemon zest and cheese.

Serve immediately.

CURRIED CAULIFLOWER

Time: 35 minutes   Servings: 4

Ingredients:

¼ cup golden raisins
1 cup boiling water
¼ cup pine nuts
½ cup olive oil, divided

1 head cauliflower, cored and cut into
1-inch pieces
1 tablespoon curry powder
Salt, to taste

Directions:

Preheat the Airfryer to 390 degrees F.
Soak the raisins in boiling water and keep aside.
In a bowl, add pine nuts and1 teaspoon of olive oil and toss to coat.
Place pine nuts in the Airfryer and cook for about 1-2 minutes.
Remove from the Airfryer and keep aside to cool.
In a bowl, mix together cauliflower, remaining oil, curry powder and salt.
Place half of the cauliflower in the Airfryer.
Cook for about 8-10 minutes.
Repeat with the remaining cauliflower.
Drain the golden raisins into a strainer.
In a bowl, add cauliflower, raisins and pine nuts and toss to coat.
Serve warm.

CAULIFLOWER WITH CREAMY WHISKEY SAUCE

Time: 30 minutes   Servings: 2

Ingredients:

1 medium head cauliflower
1 tablespoon olive oil
Salt and freshly ground black pepper, to
taste
1 tablespoon unsalted butter

2 tablespoons onion, chopped finely
2 tablespoons whiskey
¼ teaspoon vegetable stock cube, crushed
¼ cup water
¼ cup low fat cream

Directions:

Core the cauliflower and the cut the cauliflower in half, directly through the center.
Cut the cauliflower in thick slice.
In a bowl of salted warm, soak the cauliflower slices for about 15 minutes.
Rinse well.
In a pan of boiling water, cook the cauliflower slices for about 3-4 minutes.
Drain well and transfer in a bowl of cold water.
Drain well and with paper towels, dry the cauliflower slices completely.
Preheat the air fryer to 375 degrees F
In a bowl, add cauliflower slices, olive oil, salt and pepper and toss to coat.

Arrange the cauliflower slices in an Airfryer basket.

Cook for about 5 minutes.

For sauce, in a pan, melt the butter on medium heat.

Add onion and sauté for 5 about minutes.

Reduce the heat to low and stir in the whiskey.

Simmer for about 3-4 minutes.

Add the stock cube and simmer for about 3 minutes more.

Add cream and simmer for about 5 minutes.

Season with salt and pepper and remove from heat.

Pour sauce over cauliflower slices and serve.

Cauliflower with Buffalo Sauce

Time: 25 minutes   Servings: 6

Ingredients:

1 large head cauliflower, cut into bite-size florets

Olive oil, as required

2 teaspoons garlic powder

Salt and freshly ground black pepper, to taste

1 tablespoon butter, melted

2/3 cup warm buffalo wing style hot sauce

Directions:

Preheat the air fryer to 450 degrees F.

In a large bowl, add cauliflower florets, olive oil, garlic powder, salt and pepper and toss to coat.

Preheat the air fryer to 375 degrees F.

Arrange the cauliflower florets in an Airfryer basket.

Cook for about 6-7 minutes.

Remove from Airfryer and cot the cauliflower florets with buffalo wing sauce.

Cook in the Airfryer for about 5 minutes more.

Spiced Butternut Squash

Time: 30 minutes   Servings: 4

Ingredients:

1 medium butternut squash, peeled, seeded and cut into chunk

2 teaspoons cumin seeds

1/8 teaspoon garlic powder

1/8 teaspoon chili flakes, crushed

Salt and freshly ground black pepper, to taste

1 tablespoon olive oil

2 tablespoons pine nuts

2 tablespoons fresh cilantro, chopped

Directions:

In a bowl, add squash, spices and oil and toss to coat well.

Preheat the air fryer to 375 degrees F.

Arrange the butternut squash chunks in an Airfryer basket.

Cook for about 20 minutes, flipping occasionally.
Serve with the garnishing of cilantro.

WINE FLAVORED MUSHROOMS

Time: 45 minutes   Servings: 2

Ingredients:

2 teaspoons herbs de Provence   2 pounds mushrooms, quartered
½ teaspoon garlic powder   2 tablespoons white vermouth
1 tablespoon butter

Directions:

Preheat the Airfryer to 320 degrees F.
In an air fryer pan, mix together herbs de Provence, garlic powder and butter and cook for about 2 minutes.
Add mushrooms and cook for about 25 minutes.
Add white vermouth and cook for 5 minutes more.

CHEESY MUSHROOMS

Time: 20 minutes   Servings: 4

Ingredients:

6-ounce button mushrooms, stemmed   2 tablespoons mozzarella cheese, grated
2 tablespoons olive oil   2 tablespoons cheddar cheese, grated
2 tablespoons Italian dried mixed herbs 1 teaspoon dried dill
Salt and freshly ground black pepper, to
taste

Directions:

Wash and trim thin slices from the ends of the stems.
In a bowl, mix together mushrooms, Italian dried mixed herbs, oil, salt and pepper.
Preheat the air fryer to 355 degrees F.
Place the mushrooms in a fryer basket, hollow part upwards.
Top with both cheeses
Cook for about 8 minutes.
Sprinkle with dried dill and serve.

MINI MUSHROOM PIZZAS

Time: 20 minutes   Servings: 2

Ingredients:

2 Portabella caps, stemmed   Salt, to taste
2 tablespoon olive oil   2 tablespoon canned tomatoes with basil
1/8 teaspoon dried Italian seasonings 2 tablespoons mozzarella cheese, shredded

4 pepperoni slices
2 tablespoons mozzarella cheese, grated freshly

1 teaspoon red pepper flakes, crushed

Directions:
Preheat the Airfryer at 320 degrees F.

With a spoon, scoop out the center of mushroom caps.

Drizzle portabella cap with oil from both sides.

Sprinkle the inside of the caps with Italian seasoning and salt.

Place the canned tomato over both caps evenly, followed by mozzarella cheese.

Place the portabella caps in Airfryer.

Cook for about 1-2 minutes.

Top with pepperoni and cook for about 3-4 minutes.

Sprinkle with Parmesan cheese and sprinkle with red pepper flakes.

Serve immediately.

SPINACH WITH BACON

Time: 20 minutes   Servings: 2

Ingredients:
2 tablespoons olive oil
3 bacon slices, chopped
1 onion, chopped

1 garlic clove, minced
4-ounce fresh spinach

Directions:
Preheat the Airfryer to 340 degrees F.

In an air fryer pan, heat the oil for about 2 minutes.

Add bacon, onion and garlic and cook for about 3 minutes.

Add spinach and cook for about 4 minutes.

LEMONY GREEN BEANS

Time: 25 minutes   Servings: 4

Ingredients:
1 pound green beans, washed and trimmed
1 teaspoon butter, melted
1 tablespoon fresh lemon juice

¼ teaspoon garlic powder
Salt and freshly ground black pepper, to taste

Directions:
Preheat the Airfryer to 400 degrees F.

In a large bowl, add all ingredients and toss to coat well.

Place the beans in Airfryer basket.

Cook for about 10-12 minutes.

CREAMY ASPARAGUS

Time: 15 minutes   Servings: 2

Ingredients:
½ pound baby asparagus, washed and pat dried
¼ cup all-purpose flour
Salt and freshly ground black pepper, to taste
1 egg
2 tablespoons breadcrumbs
¼ cup mayonnaise

Directions:
Preheat the Airfryer to 355 degrees F.
In a shallow dish, ix together flour, salt and black pepper.
In another shallow dish, crack the egg and beat slightly.
Coat the asparagus in flour mixture and then dip in egg evenly.
In a baking dish arrange a piece of foil.
Place he asparagus onto the piece of foil.
Sprinkle with breadcrumbs and drizzle with mayonnaise.
Arrange the baking dish in Airfryer.
Cook for about 5 minutes.

STUFFED OKRA

Time: 30 minutes   Servings: 2

Ingredients:
8 ounce large okra   ½ teaspoon ground turmeric
¼ cup chickpea flour   ½ teaspoon red chili powder
¼ of onion, chopped   ½ teaspoon ground cumin
2 tablespoons coconut, grated freshly Salt, to taste
1 teaspoon garam masala powder

Directions:
Preheat the Airfryer to 390 degrees F.
With a knife, make a slit in each okra vertically without cutting in 2 halves.
In a bowl, mix together remaining ingredients.
Stuff each okra with spice mixture.
Arrange the stuffed okra in an Airfryer basket.
Cook for about 12 minutes.

Stuffed Mushrooms

Time: 25 minutes   Servings: 4

Ingredients:
1½ spelt bread slices
1 garlic clove, crushed
1 tablespoon flat-leafed parsley, chopped
finely

Salt and freshly ground black pepper, to
taste
1½ tablespoon olive oil
16 small button mushrooms, stalks
removed

Directions:
Preheat the Airfryer to 390 degrees F. In a food processor, add bread slices and pulse till fine crumbs form.
Transfer the crumbs into a bowl. Add garlic, parsley, salt and stir to combine.
Stir in olive oil.
Stuff the mushroom caps with the breadcrumb mixture.
Place the mushroom caps in an Airfryer basket.
Cook for about 9-10 minutes.

Rice & Peas Stuffed Tomatoes

Time: 40 minutes   Servings: 4

Ingredients:
4 tomatoes
1 teaspoon olive oil
1 carrot, peeled and chopped
1 onion, chopped

1 cup frozen peas, thawed
1 garlic clove, minced
2 cups cold cooked rice
1 tablespoon soy sauce

Directions:
Cut the top of each tomato and scoop out pulp and seeds. In a skillet, heat oil on low heat.
Add carrot, onion, peas and garlic and cook for about 2 minutes.
Stir in soy sauce and rice and remove from heat. Preheat the Airfryer to 355 degrees F.
Stuff tomatoes with the rice mixture.
Place the tomato in an Airfryer basket.
Cook for about 20 minutes.

Cheesy Broccoli Stuffed Tomatoes

Time: 25 minutes   Servings: 2

Ingredients:
2 large tomatoes
½ cup broccoli, chopped
½ cup cheddar cheese, shredded

1 tablespoon unsalted butter, melted
½ teaspoon dried thyme, crushed

Directions:

Slice the top of each tomato and scoop out pulp and seeds.

In a bowl, mix together chopped broccoli and cheese.

Stuff each tomato with broccoli mixture evenly.

Preheat the Airfryer to 355 degrees F.

Arrange the tomatoes in an Airfryer basket.

Drizzle with butter evenly.

Cook for about 12-15 minutes.

Garnish with thyme and serve.

BEANS & OATS STUFFED BELL PEPPERS

Time: 30 minutes   Servings: 2

Ingredients:

1 large red bell pepper, halved and seeded
1 cup cooked oatmeal
2 tablespoons canned red kidney beans
2 tablespoons plain yogurt

1/8 teaspoon ground cumin
1/8 teaspoon smoked paprika
Salt and freshly ground black pepper, to taste

Directions:

Preheat the Airfryer to 355 degrees F.

In Airfryer pan, place the bell peppers, face down.

Cook for about 8 minutes.

Remove from the Airfryer and keep aside to cool.

Meanwhile in a bowl, mix together remaining ingredients.

Stuff the pepper halves with oatmeal mixture evenly.

Set the Airfryer to 355 degrees F.

Cook for about 8 minutes.

CHEESE STUFFED BELL PEPPERS

Time: 20 minutes   Servings: 4

Ingredients:

8 mini red bell peppers
½ tablespoon olive oil
1 teaspoon fresh parsley, chopped

Freshly ground black pepper, to taste
¾ cup feta cheese, crumbled

Directions:

Preheat the Airfryer to 390 degrees F. Cut the tops of the peppers and discard the seeds.

In a bowl, mix together the remaining ingredients.

Stuff the bell peppers with cheese mixture.

Arrange the bell peppers in an Airfryer basket.

Cook for about 8 minutes.

CHEESY VEGGIES STUFFED BELL PEPPERS

Time: 50 minutes   Servings: 6

Ingredients:

6 medium bell peppers
1 carrot, peeled and chopped finely
1 onion, chopped finely
1 potato, peeled and chopped finely
1 bread roll, chopped finely
2 cloves of garlic

½ cup fresh peas, shelled
2 teaspoons fresh parsley, chopped
Salt and freshly ground black pepper, to taste
1/3 cup cheddar cheese, grated

Directions:

Preheat the air fryer to 350 degrees F.
Cut the tops off the peppers and remove the seeds and pith.
In a bowl, add all ingredients except cheese and mix well.
Stuff the peppers with the vegetable mixture.
Arrange the peppers into the Airfryer.
Cook for about 20 minutes.
Now, top the peppers with cheese evenly and cook for about 5 minutes more.

STUFFED EGGPLANT

Time: 40 minutes   Servings: 2

Ingredients:

1 large eggplant
2 teaspoons olive oil, divided
2 teaspoons fresh lemon juice, divided
8 cherry tomatoes, quartered

2 tablespoons tomato salsa
½ tablespoon fresh parsley
Salt and freshly ground black pepper, to taste

Directions:

Preheat the Airfryer to 390 degrees F.
Grease the Airfryer pan.
Place eggplant in pan and cook for about 15 minutes.
Remove eggplant from Airfryer and cut in half lengthwise.
Drizzle with 1 teaspoon of oil evenly.
Now, set the Airfryer to 355 degrees F.
Cook for about 10 minutes more.
Remove eggplant from Airfryer and keep aside for about 5 minutes.
Carefully, scoop, out the flesh, leaving about ¼-inch away from edges.
Drizzle the eggplant halves with 1 teaspoon of lemon juice.
Transfer the eggplant flesh into a bowl.
Add remaining ingredients and mix well.
Stuff the eggplant haves with tomato mixture and serve.

Veggies Stuffed Pumpkin Basket

Time: 50 minutes   Servings: 6

Ingredients:
1 sweet potato, peeled and chopped
1 parsnip, peeled and chopped
1 carrot, peeled and chopped
½ cup peas, shelled
1 onion, chopped

2 garlic cloves, minced
1 egg, beaten
2 teaspoons herb mix
½ of butternut pumpkin, seeded

Directions:
In a large bowl, add all ingredients except pumpkin and mix till well combined.
Stuff the pumpkin half with the vegetable mixture. Preheat the air fryer to 355 degrees F.
Place pumpkin into the fryer basket.
Cook for about 30 minutes.

Mixed Veggies

Time: 30 minutes   Servings: 4

Ingredients:
1 green bell pepper, seeded and chopped
1 yellow bell pepper, seeded and chopped
1 eggplant, chopped
1 zucchini, chopped
3 tomatoes, chopped
2 small onions, chopped

2 garlic cloves, minced
2 tablespoons herbs de Provence
1 tablespoon olive oil
1 tablespoon balsamic vinegar
Salt and freshly ground black pepper, to taste

Directions:
Preheat the air fryer to 355 degrees F.
In a large bowl, add all ingredients and toss to coat well.
Transfer to a baking dish.
Cook for about 15 minutes, stirring once in the middle way.
After cooking, keep in the Airfryer for about 3-4 minutes to cool.

Herbed Veggies

Time: 50 minutes   Servings: 4

Ingredients:
6 teaspoons olive oil, divided
½ pound carrots, peeled and sliced
1 pound yellow squash, sliced
1 pound zucchini, sliced

Salt and freshly ground black pepper, to taste
½ tablespoon fresh basil, chopped
½ tablespoon tarragon leaves, chopped

Directions:

Preheat the air fryer at 400 degrees F. In a bowl, mix together 2 teaspoons oil and carrot.

Place the carrot in an Airfryer basket Cook for 5 about minutes.

Meanwhile in a large bowl, mix together remaining 4 teaspoons of oil, yellow squash, zucchini, salt and white pepper.

Transfer the zucchini mixture in Airfryer basket with carrots.

Cook for about 30 minutes, tossing 2-3 times.

Place into the serving bowl.

Add tarragon leaves and mix till well combined.

MARINATED TOFU

Time: 45 minutes   Servings: 4

Ingredients:

2 tablespoons low-sodium soy sauce
2 tablespoons fish sauce
1 teaspoon sesame oil
1 teaspoon chicken bouillon granules

12-ounce extra-firm tofu, drained and cubed into 1-inch size
1 teaspoon butter

Directions:

In a large bowl, add soy sauce, fish sauce, sesame oil and chicken granules and mix till well combined.

Add tofu cubes and toss to coat well.

Keep aside to marinate for about 30 minutes, tossing occasionally.

Preheat the air fryer to 355 degrees F.

Place the tofu cubes in an Airfryer basket.

Cook for about 25-30 minutes, flipping after every 10 minutes.

FLOUR CRUSTED TOFU

Time: 25 minutes   Servings: 2

Ingredients:

1 block firm tofu, drained and cubed into ½-inch size
2 tablespoons cornstarch
¼ cup rice flour

Salt and freshly ground black pepper, to taste
2 tablespoons olive oil

Directions:

Preheat the Airfryer to 360 degrees F.

In a bowl mix together cornstarch, rice flour, salt and black pepper.

Coat the tofu with flour mixture evenly.

Drizzle the tofu with oil evenly.

Arrange the tofu in an Airfryer basket.

Cook for about 14 minutes preside.

VEGGIE PIZZA

Time: 30 minutes

Servings: 4

Ingredients:

For Sauce:

1¼ cups tomato sauce
1/8 teaspoon dried oregano, crushed
1/8 teaspoon dried basil, crushed
Granulated garlic, to taste
Granulated onion, to taste
Salt and freshly ground black pepper, to taste
Pinch of sugar

For Pizza:

Flour, as required
1 frozen pizza dough
3-4 fresh mushroom, sliced
1 red bell pepper, seeded and chopped
3-4 fresh basil leaves
1/8 teaspoon dried oregano, crushed
¼ cup mozzarella cheese, grated

Directions:

For sauce in a bowl, mix together all ingredients. Keep aside.
Sprinkle some flour onto a smooth surface.
Coat the dough ball in flour and knead well.
Make a 5-inch circle of dough for your crust.
Preheat the air fryer at 400 degrees F.
Grease a baking pan generously.
Spread sauce over crust evenly.
Top with mushrooms, bell pepper and basil leaves.
Sprinkle with oregano evenly.
Cook for about 8 minutes.
Remove from Airfryer and top with cheese evenly.
Cook for about 5 minutes more.
Cut into desired size wedges and serve.

SIMPLE BEEF BURGERS

Time: 25 minutes

Servings: 3

Ingredients:

1 pound ground beef
Salt and freshly ground black pepper, to taste

6 cheddar cheese slices
6 dinner rolls
3 tablespoons tomato ketchup

Directions:

Preheat the Airfryer to 390 degrees F.
Grease an Airfryer pan
In a bowl, mix together beef, salt and black pepper.
Make small 6 patties from mixture.

Place patties onto the prepared pan.
Cook for about 10-11 minutes.
Place 1 cheese slice on top of each patty.
Arrange patties between rolls.
Top with ketchup and serve.

CHEESY BEEF BURGERS

Time: 25 minutes   Servings: 2

Ingredients:
1 tablespoon olive oil
½ pound ground beef
1 garlic clove, minced
2 tablespoons fresh cilantro, minced
2 tablespoons olive oil

Salt and freshly ground black pepper, to taste
2 cheddar cheese slices
2 salad leaves
2 dinner roll, cut into half

Directions:
Preheat the Airfryer to 390 degrees F.
Grease the Airfryer pan with olive oil.
In a bowl, add beef, garlic, cilantro, salt and black pepper and mix well.
Make 2 (4-inch) patties from the mixture.
Place patties onto the prepared pan.
Cook for about 10-11 minutes.
Place 1 cheese slices over each patty and cook for about 1 minute more.
Arrange 1 salad leaf between each diner roll.
Top with 1 patty and serve.

HERBED PORK BURGERS

Time: 60 minutes   Servings: 4

Ingredients:
10 ½-ounce ground pork
1 small onion, chopped
1teaspoon garlic puree
1 teaspoon tomato puree
1 teaspoon mustard
1 teaspoon fresh basil, chopped

1 teaspoon dried mixed herbs, crushed
Salt and freshly ground black pepper, to taste
¼ cup cheddar cheese, grated
4 burger buns

Directions:
In a bowl add all ingredients except cheese and buns and mix well.
Make 4 medium sized patties from mixture.
Preheat the Airfryer to 390 degrees F.
Grease the Airfryer pan with olive oil.

Place patties onto the prepared pan.

Cook for about 45 minutes, flipping once after 25 minutes.

Arrange the patties in buns with cheese and serve.

CHEESY TURKEY BURGERS

Time: 25 minutes   Servings: 4

Ingredients:

1½ pounds lean ground turkey
1 tablespoon Worcestershire sauce
1 tablespoon Montreal steak seasoning

½ cup store-bought or homemade cheese sauce
1 cup shredded Cheddar cheese
Onion hamburger rolls, toasted

Directions:

Preheat the Airfryer to 370 degrees F.

In a bowl, add turkey, Worcestershire sauce and Montreal steak seasoning and mix till well combined.

Make 4 equal sized patties from mixture.

Place the burgers into the air fryer basket.

Cook for about 16 minutes, flipping once in half way.

In a bowl, mix together cheese sauce and Cheddar cheese.

Spoon ¼ of the cheese mixture over each burger and cook for about 4minutes more.

Serve the burgers on toasted onion rolls.

COD BURGERS WITH SALSA

Time: 35 minutes   Servings: 6

Ingredients:

For Mango Salsa:
3 cups mango, peeled, pitted and cubed
1 tablespoon fresh parsley, chopped
1 teaspoon fresh lime zest, grated finely
½ teaspoon red chili paste
1 tablespoon fresh lime juice
For Cod Cakes:
1 pound cod fillets

1 teaspoon fresh lime zest, grated finely
1 egg
1 teaspoon red chili paste
Salt, to taste
1 tablespoon fresh lime juice
1/3 cup coconut, grated and divided
1 scallion, chopped finely
2 tablespoons fresh parsley, chopped

Directions:

For salsa in a bowl, mix together all ingredients.

Refrigerate till serving.

For cod cakes in a food processor, add cod filets, lime zest, egg, chili paste, salt and lime juice and pulse till smooth.

Transfer the cod mixture into a bowl.

Add 2 tablespoons coconut, scallion and parsley and mix till well combined.

Make 12 equal sized round cakes from the mixture.
In a shallow dish, place the remaining coconut.
Coat the cod cakes in coconut evenly.
Preheat the air fryer to 375 degrees F.
Arrange 6 cakes in an Airfryer basket and cook for about 7 minutes.
Repeat with the remaining cod cakes.
Serve these cod cakes with mango salsa.

SALMON & VEGGIE BURGERS

Time: 45 minutes   Servings: 6

Ingredients:

3 large russet potatoes, peeled and cubed
1 (6-ounce) salmon fillet
1 egg
¾ cup frozen vegetables (of your choice), parboiled and drained
2 tablespoons fresh parsley, chopped

1 teaspoon fresh dill, chopped
Salt and freshly ground black pepper, to taste
1 cup breadcrumbs
¼ cup olive oil

Directions:

In a pan of boiling water, cook the potatoes for about 10 minutes.
Drain well.
Transfer to the bowl and mash with a potato masher.
Keep aside to cool completely.
Preheat the air fryer to 355 degrees F.
Place fish into the fryer basket.
Cook the salmon fillet for about 5 minutes.
Transfer the salmon into a large bowl and flake with a fork.
Add cooked potatoes, egg, parboiled vegetables, parsley, dill, salt and black pepper and mix till well combined.
Make 6 equal sized patties from the mixture.
Coat patties with breadcrumb evenly and then drizzle with the oil evenly.
Transfer the patties into the fryer basket
Preheat the air fryer to 355 degrees F.
Line the pan with foil paper.
Arrange the patties into prepared pan.
Cook for 10-12 minutes, flipping once in the middle way.

LEMONY TUNA BURGERS

Time: 25 minutes   Servings: 8

Ingredients:

2 (6-ounce) cans tuna, drained
½ cup panko bread crumbs

1 egg
2 teaspoons Dijon mustard

2 tablespoons fresh parsley, chopped
Dash of Tabasco sauce
Salt and freshly ground black pepper, to taste

1 tablespoon fresh lemon juice
1 tablespoon olive oil

Directions:

In a large bowl, add all ingredients and mix till well combined.
Make equal sized patties from the mixture and arrange onto a foil paper lined tray.
Refrigerate for overnight
Preheat the air fryer to 355 degrees F.
Place the patties in an Airfryer basket.
Cook for about 10 minutes.

PRAWN BURGERS

Time: 25 minutes   Servings: 2

Ingredients:

½ cup prawns, peeled, deveined and chopped very finely
½ cup breadcrumbs
2-3 tablespoons onion, chopped finely
½ teaspoon ginger, minced
½ teaspoon garlic, minced

½ teaspoon red chili powder
½ teaspoon ground cumin
¼ teaspoon ground turmeric
Salt and freshly ground black pepper, to taste

Directions:

In a bowl, sad all ingredients and mix till well combined.
Preheat the Airfryer to 390 degrees F.
Make small sized patties from mixture.
Now, set the Airfryer to 355 degrees F.
Arrange the patties in Airfryer.
Cook for about 5-6 minutes.

HONEY MUSTARD CHEESY MEATBALLS

Time: 30 minutes   Servings: 4

Ingredients:

½ pound ground beef
1 onion, chopped
1 teaspoon garlic paste
2 tablespoons fresh basil, chopped
1 teaspoon mustard

1 teaspoon honey
1 tablespoon cheddar cheese, grated
Salt and freshly ground black pepper, to taste

Directions:

Preheat the Airfryer to 390 degrees F.

In a bowl, add all ingredients and mix till well combined.

Make small equal-sized balls from the mixture.

Arrange the balls in an Airfryer basket.

Cook for about 14 minutes or till golden browned.

Serve with fresh greens.

$\mathcal{H}$ERBED MEATBALLS

Time: 30 minutes   Servings: 4

Ingredients:

1 pound ground beef
½ cup onion, chopped
¾ cup panko breadcrumbs
¾ cup Parmesan cheese, grated
1 egg
1 teaspoon Italian seasoning

½ teaspoon garlic powder
2 tablespoons fresh parsley, chopped
2 tablespoons fresh cilantro, chopped
3 long hoagie rolls
Marinara sauce
8 ounce Provolone cheese slices

Directions:

Preheat the air fryer to 380 degrees F.

In a bowl, add beef, onion, breadcrumbs, Parmesan cheese, egg, Italian seasoning, garlic powder, parsley and cilantro and mix till well combined.

Make 10 equal sized meatballs from mixture.

Arrange the seatbacks in Airfryer.

Cook for about 10 minutes turning, once in the middle way.

Slice open the hoagie rolls and spread a little marinara sauce inside.

Place two slices of the Provolone cheese over the sauce.

Top the cheese with three meatballs per hoagie roll and a little additional sauce.

Top with two more slices of Provolone cheese.

Return the sandwiches to the air fryer, one or two at a time.

Cook for about 2-3 minutes more.

$\mathcal{S}$WEET & SOUR MEATBALLS

Time: 30 minutes   Servings: 8

Ingredients:

1 pound ground beef
¾ cup ketchup
1 tablespoon Tabasco sauce
2½ tablespoons Worcestershire sauce
¼ cup balsamic vinegar

1 tablespoon fresh lemon juice
½ cup brown sugar
½ teaspoon dry mustard
Fresh greens, for serving

Directions:

In a large bowl, add all ingredients except greens and mix till well combined.

Make medium sized balls from the mixture.
Place the balls in air fryer.
Preheat the Airfryer to 400 degrees F.
Arrange the balls in Airfryer.
Cook for about 15 minutes.
Serve balls with fresh greens.

CHINESE STYLE MEATBALLS

Time: 15 minutes   Servings: 6

Ingredients:
10½-ounce ground pork
1 egg, beaten
1 tablespoon light soy sauce
2 teaspoons oyster sauce
1 teaspoon sesame oil

½ teaspoon five spice powder
½ teaspoon brown sugar
½ cup cornstarch
1 tablespoon olive oil

Directions:
In a large bowl, add all ingredients except cornstarch and oil and mix till well combined.
Make small 18 equal sized balks from the mixture. In a shallow dish, place the cornstarch.
Roll the meatballs into cornstarch mixture evenly.
In a large tray, place the meatballs and keep aside for about 15 minutes.
Preheat the Airfryer to 390 degrees F. Line the Airfryer basket with foil paper.
Arrange the balls into prepared basket.
Cook for about 10 minutes.
Now, drizzle the meatballs with oil and flip the side.
Cook for about 10 minutes more.

SAUSAGE MEATBALLS

Time: 30 minutes   Servings: 4

Ingredients:
3½-ounce sausage, casing removed
½ teaspoon garlic, minced
½ medium onion, minced finely
1 teaspoon fresh sage, chopped finely

3 tablespoons Italian breadcrumbs
Salt and freshly ground black pepper, to taste

Directions:
In a bowl, add all ingredients and mix till well combined.
Make medium sized balls from the mixture.
Preheat the Airfryer to 355 degrees F.
place the balls in the Air Fryer
Cook for about 15 minutes.

CHEESY MACARONI BITES

Time: 75 minutes   Servings: 2

Ingredients:

2 cups leftover mac and cheese
1/3 cup shredded sharp cheddar cheese
3 Eggs

2 cups milk
2/3 cup all-purpose flour
1 cup breadcrumbs

Directions:

In a bowl, add leftover mac and cheese and cheddar and mix well. Keep side.

In a shallow dish, place the flour.

In a second shallow dish, add milk and eggs and beat well.

In a third shallow dish, add breadcrumbs.

Dust your hands with flour, shape the mixture into small balls.

Coat the balls with flour, then dip into egg and milk mixture.

Then coat generously with breadcrumbs.

Preheat the Airfryer to 360 degrees F.

Place the balls in Airfryer.

Cook for about 10-15 minutes.

MIRIN COATED CHICKEN KEBABS

Time: 25 minutes   Servings: 4

Ingredients:

¼ cup light soy sauce
1 tablespoon mirin
1 teaspoon garlic salt
1 teaspoon sugar

4 (4-ounce) skinless, boneless chicken
thighs, cubed into 1-inch size
5 scallions, cut into 1-inch pieces
lengthwise

Directions:

In a large baking dish, mix together soy sauce, mirin, garlic salt and sugar.

Thread chicken and green onion onto pre-soaked wooden skewers.

Place the skewers into the baking dish and coat with marinade generously.

Refrigerate, covered for about 3 hours.

Preheat the air fryer to 355 degrees F.

Place the skewers in a fryer basket.

Cook for about 10-12 minutes.

Sweet & Soy Sauce Marinated Chicken Kebabs

Time: 25 minutes   Servings: 4

Ingredients:

4 scallions, chopped
1 tablespoon fresh ginger, grated finely
4 garlic cloves, minced
½ cup pineapple juice
½ cup soy sauce

¼ cup sesame oil
Pinch of black pepper
2 teaspoons sesame seeds, toasted
1 pound chicken tenders

Directions:

In a large baking dish, mix together all ingredients except chicken.
Thread chicken onto skewer.
Add the skewers in baking dish and coat with marinade evenly.
Cover and refrigerator for about 2 hours or overnight.
Preheat the Airfryer to 390 degrees F.
Place the chicken skewers in an Airfryer basket in batches.
Cook for about 5-7 minutes.
Repeat with the remaining skewers.

Spicy Lamb Kebabs

Time: 30 minutes   Servings: 3

Ingredients:

½ pound ground lamb
2 eggs, beaten
2 garlic cloves, minced
½ cup pistachios, chopped
1 tablespoon fresh lemon juice
2 tablespoons plain flour
1 teaspoon chili flakes
1 teaspoon cumin seeds

½ teaspoon coriander seeds
½ teaspoon fennel seeds
2 tablespoons chopped flat-leaf parsley
1 teaspoon dried mint
1 teaspoon salt
½ teaspoon freshly ground black pepper
Olive oil

Directions:

In a bowl, mix together lamb, eggs, pistachios, lemon juice, flour, chili flakes, cumin seeds, coriander seeds, fennel seeds, parsley, mint, salt and pepper.
Mold handfuls of the lamb mixture to form sausages around skewers.
Brush lamb skewers with olive oil.
Preheat the air fryer to 355 degrees F.
Place the lamb skewer in a fryer grill.
Cook for about 8 minutes per side.

*V*EGGIE KEBABS

Time: 40 minutes   Servings: 6

Ingredients:

¼ cup carrots, peeled and chopped
¼ cup French beans
½ cup green peas
1 teaspoon ginger
3 garlic cloves, peeled
3 green chilies
¼ cup fresh mint leaves

½ cup cottage cheese
2 medium boiled potatoes, mashed
½ teaspoon five spice powder
Salt, to taste
2 tablespoons corn flour
Oil for brushing

Directions:

In a food processor, add carrot, beans, peas, ginger, garlic, mint, cheese and pulse till smooth.
Transfer the mixture into a bowl.
Add potato, five spice powder, salt and corn flour and mix till well combined.
Divide into equal sized small balls.
Take each ball and press around a skewer in a sausage shape.
Preheat the Airfryer to 390 degrees F.
Place the skewers in an Airfryer basket.
Brush with oil on both sides.
Cook for about 10 minutes.

*T*ATER TOTS

Time: 20 minutes   Servings: 4

Ingredients:

1 large bag extra crispy frozen tater tots
16-ounce bacon slices
½ cup cheddar cheese, shredded

4 scallions, chopped
3 tablespoons sour cream

Directions:

Wrap each tater tot with a piece of bacon
Place in Airfryer basket in batches.
Preheat the Airfryer to 400 degrees F.
Cook for about 8 minutes.
Transfer tater tots into serving plates.
Top with cheese and scallions.
Serve with sour cream

DUCK WONTON WRAPPERS

Time: 20 minutes   Servings: 12

Ingredients:

2-ounce cooked duck breast, chopped
finely
1 large celery stalk, chopped finely
¼ of red onion
2 teaspoons fresh gingerroot, grated finely
2 tablespoons tamari

2 teaspoons sesame oil
1 teaspoon chili oil
1 tablespoon rice vinegar
24 wonton skins
Canola oil spray

Directions:

In a bowl, add all ingredients except wonton skins and mix till well combined.

Place the wonton skins onto a smooth surface.

Place the filling over each wonton skin evenly.

With your wet fingers, fold on the diagonal and press to seal edges.

Then fold the two longer edges toward each other and seal with the help of wet finger.

Preheat the Airfryer to 390 degrees F.

Arrange the rolls into Airfryer basket in batches.

Cook for about 3 minutes.

Shake the basket and cook for about 2-3 minutes more.

CRAB WONTON WRAPPERS

Time: 20 minutes   Servings: 4

Ingredients:

2 (8-ounce) packages cream cheese,
softened
¼ cup sour cream
½ of onion, minced

1 tablespoon garlic powder
2 tablespoons sugar
1 pound imitation crabmeat, flaked
1 (14-ounce) package wonton wrappers

Directions:

In a bowl, add cream cheese, sour cream, onion, garlic powder and sugar and beat till smooth.

Gently, stir in the flaked imitation crab meat.

Place the wonton skins onto a smooth surface.

Place the crab filling over each wonton skin evenly.

With your wet fingers, fold on the diagonal and press to seal edges.

Then fold the two longer edges toward each other and seal with the help of wet finger.

Preheat the Airfryer to 390 degrees F.

Arrange the rolls into Airfryer basket in batches.

Cook for about 5-6 minutes, flipping once in the middle way.

BEEF & VEGGIE SPRING ROLLS

Time: 55 minutes   Servings: 10

Ingredients:

2-ounce Asian rice noodles
1 tablespoon sesame oil
7-ounce ground beef
1 small onion, chopped
3 garlic cloves, crushed

1 cup fresh mixed vegetables
1 teaspoon soy sauce
1 packet spring roll skins
2 tablespoons water
Olive oil, as required

Directions:

Soak the noodles in warm water till soft.

Drain and cut into small lengths.

In a pan heat the oil and add the onion and garlic and sauté for about 4-5 minutes.

Add beef and cook for about 4-5 minutes.

Add vegetables and cook for about 5-7 minutes or till cooked through.

Stir in soy sauce and remove from the heat.

Immediately, stir in the noodles and keep aside till all the juices have been absorbed.

Preheat the air fryer to 350 degrees F.

Preheat the oven to 350 degrees F also.

Place the spring rolls skin onto a smooth surface.

Add a line of the filling diagonally across.

Fold the top point over the filling and then fold in both sides.

On the final point brush it with water before rolling to seal.

Brush the spring rolls with oil.

Arrange the rolls in batches in Airfryer.

Cook for about 8 minutes.

Repeat with remaining rolls.

Now, place spring rolls onto a baking sheet.

Bake for about 6 minutes per side

CHICKEN & VEGGIE SPRING ROLLS

Time: 20 minutes   Servings: 4

Ingredients:

¾ cup cooked chicken breast, shredded
1 celery stalk, chopped
¼ cup carrot, peeled and chopped finely
¼ cup fresh mushrooms, chopped finely
½ teaspoon fresh ginger, chopped finely
1 teaspoon sugar
1 teaspoon chicken stock powder

1 egg
1 teaspoon corn starch
8 spring roll wrappers
Olive oil, as required

Directions:

In a large bowl, add chicken, celery, carrot, mushroom, ginger, sugar and chicken stock powder and mix till well combined.

In another bowl, add egg, corn starch and beat till a thick paste forms. Keep aside.

Arrange the spring rolls onto smooth surface.

Place some filling onto each spring roll wrapper and roll it up.

Seal the ends with the egg mixture.

Lightly brush the spring rolls with oil.

Preheat the Airfryer to 390 degrees F.

Place the rolls into the Airfryer basket.

Cook for about 4 minutes.

PRAWN SPRING ROLLS

Time: 25 minutes   Servings: 4

Ingredients:

1 tablespoon olive oil,
1 teaspoon fresh gingerroot, minced
3½-ounce fresh mushrooms, sliced
1 tablespoon soy sauce
1-ounce tinned water chestnuts, sliced
1 teaspoon Chinese five-spice powder
1-ounce beansprouts

1 scallion, chopped
1 small carrot, peeled and cut into matchsticks
3½-ounce cooked prawns
12 spring roll wrappers,
1 egg, beaten

Directions:

In a skillet, heat oil on medium heat.

Add ginger, mushrooms and water chestnuts and sauté for about 2 minutes.

Stir in the soy sauce, five-spice powder, beansprouts, scallion and carrot and cook for about 1 minute.

Remove from heat and keep aside to cool.

Then, stir in the prawns. Arrange the spring rolls onto smooth surface.

Place some filling onto each spring roll wrapper and roll it up.

Seal the ends with the egg.

Preheat the Airfryer to 390 degrees F.

Place the rolls into the Airfryer basket.

Cook for about 5 minutes.

BELL PEPPER ROLLS

Time: 25 minutes   Servings: 8

Ingredients:

2 medium red bell peppers
2 medium yellow bell peppers
2 medium orange bell peppers

½ cup Greek feta cheese, crumbled
1 scallion, sliced thinly
2 tablespoons fresh oregano, chopped

Directions:

Preheat the Airfryer to 390 degrees F. Arrange the bell peppers in Airfryer basket.

Cook for about 10 minutes. Meanwhile in a bowl, mix together all ingredients.

Remove the peppers from Airfryer.

Cut the bell peppers in half lengthwise and remove the seeds.

Place the filling over cut side and roll up, starting from the narrowest end.

Secure each roll with toothpick.

CREAMY TURKEY & APPLE SANDWICH

Time: 25 minutes   Servings: 6

Ingredients:

1½ cups cream cheese, softened
¾ cup mayonnaise
1 teaspoon curry powder
4 medium apples, cored and sliced thinly

1 standard loaf of bread, crust removed and sliced
4 cups smoked turkey breast, sliced

Directions:

In a bowl, add cream cheese, mayonnaise and curry powder and mix till smooth.

Brush the apple slices with some cream cheese mixture.

Spread the cream cheese mixture on two slices of bread.

Arrange the apple slices and then turkey slices on one slice of bread.

Cover with a second slice of bread. Prepare the remaining sandwich in the same manner.

Preheat the Airfryer to 360 degrees F.

Arrange the sandwich in Airfryer.

Cook for about 5-7 minutes.

CHEESY TURKEY SANDWICH

Time: 15 minutes   Servings: 2

Ingredients:

2 tablespoon butter
8 cooked turkey breast slices
4 rye bread slices
8 Swiss cheese slices

2 tablespoon salad dressing (of your choice)
4 tablespoon coleslaw

Directions:

Spread butter on one side of each bread slice Arrange butter-side down on cutting board.

On each piece place cheese, followed by turkey, dressing and coleslaw.

Butter other slice of bread and place on top of sandwich filling.

Preheat the Airfryer to 310 degrees F.

Place the sandwiches into Airfryer basket.

Cook for about 6 minutes.

PROSCIUTTO SANDWICH

Time: 30 minutes

Servings: 1

Ingredients:

2 bread slices
2 prosciutto slices
2 tomato slices
2 mozzarella cheese slices

2 fresh basil leaves
Pinch of salt and freshly ground black pepper
1 tablespoon olive oil

Directions:

Place bread slice onto smooth surface.
Place prosciutto over 1 bread slice, followed cheese slices.
Preheat the Airfryer to 390 degrees F.
Arrange the sandwich in Airfryer basket.
Cook for about 5 minutes.
Remove the sandwich from Airfryer.
Drizzle with olive oil and sprinkle with salt and pepper.
Top with tomato and basil and serve.

CHEESY VEGGIE SANDWICH

Time: 30 minutes

Servings: 2

Ingredients:

1 tablespoon olive oil
1/3 cup asparagus, trimmed and cut in 1-inch pieces
1/3 cup fresh mushrooms, sliced thinly
Salt and freshly ground black pepper, to taste

4 white bread slices
½ cup sharp cheddar cheese, grated
¼ cup butter, melted
1/3 cup fresh spinach leaves, torn
2 tablespoons roasted red peppers, chopped

Directions:

In a non-stick pan, heat oil on med-high heat.
Add asparagus, and mushrooms and sauté for about 5 minutes.
Season with the salt and pepper.
Place cheese and butter in separate bowls.
Brush the butter on each side of the 4 bread slices.
Place the cheese over 2 bread slices.
Place the sautéed mushrooms, asparagus, roasted red peppers and fresh spinach leaves over the cheese.
Cover with remaining slices.
Preheat the Airfryer to 360 degrees F.
Arrange the sandwich in Airfryer.
Cook for about 5-7 minutes.

Dinner Recipes

Mexican Style Chicken

Time: 45 minutes   Servings: 4

Ingredients:

1 (8-ounce) skinless, boneless chicken breast
2 bay leaves
1 small yellow onion, chopped
3 garlic cloves, chopped
½ of poblano pepper
1 (14½-ounce) can diced tomatoes

1 (10-ounce) can rotel tomatoes
Salt, to taste
10 corn tortillas, cut into diamond slices
1 tablespoon olive oil
4 tablespoons feta cheese, crumbled
¼ cup sour cream
2 red onions, sliced

Directions:

In a pan of water, add the chicken and bay leaves and cook for about 20 minutes.
Transfer chicken breasts in a bowl and keep aside to cool.
With 2 forks, shred the chicken.
In a food processor, add onion, garlic, poblano pepper and both cans of tomato and pulse till smooth.
Transfer the sauce into a skillet on medium-high heat and bring to a boil.
Reduce the heat to medium-low and simmer for about 10 minutes.
Stir in the salt and remove from the heat and keep aside.
Preheat the Airfryer to 400 degrees F.
In a bowl, add half of tortilla slices, half of oil and salt and toss to coat well.
Place the tortilla slices in an Airfryer basket.
Cook for about 10 minutes.
Repeat with the remaining tortillas.
Transfer the tortillas into the serving bowl.
Add sauce, cheese and sour cream and mix.
Top with the red onion and chicken and serve.

Asian Style Chicken

Time: 35 minutes   Servings: 2

Ingredients:

¾ pound chicken pieces
1 teaspoon ginger, minced
1 tablespoon soy sauce
½ tablespoon olive oil
1 tablespoon fresh rosemary, chopped
1 tablespoon oyster sauce

3 tablespoons brown sugar
1 lemon, cut into wedges

Directions:

In a bowl, mix together chicken, ginger, soy sauce and olive oil.

Cover and refrigerator for about 30 minutes.

Preheat the Airfryer to 390 degrees F.

Place the chicken in an Airfryer pan.

Cook for about 6 minutes.

Meanwhile in a small bowl, mix together the remaining ingredients.

Remove baking pan from the Airfryer.

Spread rosemary mixture over chicken.

Squeeze some juice from lemon wedges over chicken.

Place the wedges on top.

Cook for about 13 minutes.

CHICKEN DRUMSTICKS WITH PANDAN

Time: 25 minutes   Servings: 2

Ingredients:

1 tablespoon oyster sauce
2 tablespoons maltose
1½ tablespoons fish sauce
1 teaspoon sugar
1/3 teaspoon dark soy sauce
½ teaspoon garlic powder

½ teaspoon onion powder
¼ teaspoon ground turmeric
3 boneless chicken drumsticks, cut into small pieces
12-14 pandan leaves
1 tablespoon olive oil

Directions:

In a bowl, mix together all ingredients except chicken and pandan leaves.

Add chicken and coat with marinade generously.

Refrigerate to marinate for at least 4 hours.

Wrap the chicken pieces with pandan leaves.

Drizzle wrapped chicken with some oil and toss.

Preheat the Airfryer to 390 degrees F.

Place chicken into an Airfryer baking tray.

Cook for about 7 minutes.

Flip the side and cook for about 5 minutes more

HONEY GLAZED CHICKEN DRUMSTICKS

Time: 35 minutes   Servings: 4

Ingredients:

¼ cup Dijon mustard
1 tablespoon honey
2 tablespoons olive oil
½ tablespoon fresh rosemary, minced

1 tablespoon fresh thyme, minced
Salt and freshly ground black pepper, to taste

4 boneless chicken drumsticks Marinated the chicken drumsticks with all the above ingredients for overnight.Preheat Philips Airfryer at 160 degree.
Baked the drumstick for 12 minutes at 160 degree. Then baked for 5 to 10 minutes at 180 degree for crispy skin.

Directions:

In a bowl, add all ingredients except the drumsticks and mix till well combined.

Add drumsticks and coat with the mixture generously.

Refrigerate, covered o marinate for overnight.

Preheat the Airfryer at 320 degrees F.

Place the drumsticks in a fryer basket.

Cook for about 12 minutes.

Now, set the air fryer to 355 degrees F.

Cook for about 5-10 minutes.

SWEET & SPICY CHICKEN DRUMSTICKS

Time: 20 minutes

Servings: 4

Ingredients:

1 teaspoon cayenne pepper
1 teaspoon chili powder
1 garlic clove, crushed
2 teaspoons brown sugar
1 tablespoon mustard

Salt and freshly ground black pepper, to taste
1 tablespoon vegetable oil
4 chicken drumsticks

Directions:

Preheat the Airfryer to 390 degrees F.

In a bowl, mix together all ingredients except chicken drumsticks.

Rub the chicken with the oil mix and refrigerate to marinate for about 20-30 minutes.

Place each drumstick in an Airfryer basket.

Cook for about 10 minutes.

Now, set the Airfryer to 300 degrees F.

Cook for about 10 minutes.

CHINESE STYLE CHICKEN DRUMSTICKS

Time: 30 minutes

Servings: 4

Ingredients:

1 tablespoon oyster sauce
1 teaspoon light soy sauce
½ teaspoon sesame oil
1 teaspoon Chinese five spice powder

Salt and freshly ground white pepper, to taste
4 chicken drumsticks
Corn flour, as required

Directions:

In a large bowl, mix together all ingredients except drumsticks and corn flour.

Add chicken drumsticks and coat with marinade generously.

Refrigerate for at least 30-40 minutes.

In a shallow dish, place the corn flour.

Remove the chicken from marinade and coat with corn flour slightly and shake off the excess.

Preheat the Airfryer to 390 degrees F.

Place each drumstick in an Airfryer basket.

Cook for about 20 minutes.

GINGERED CHICKEN DRUMSTICKS

Time: 40 minutes   Servings: 3

Ingredients:

¼ cup full-fat coconut milk
2 teaspoons fresh ginger, minced
2 teaspoons galangal, minced

2 teaspoons ground turmeric
Salt, to taste
3 chicken drumsticks

Directions:

In a bowl, mix together all ingredients except chicken drumsticks.

Add chicken drumsticks and coat with marinade generously.

Refrigerate to marinate for at least 6-8 hours.

Preheat the Airfryer at 375 degrees F.

Place the chicken in Airfryer.

Cook for about 20-25 minutes.

CRUSTED CHICKEN THIGHS

Time: 45 minutes   Servings: 2

Ingredients:

3 shallots, chopped finely
2 tablespoons light soy sauce
1/8 teaspoon freshly ground white pepper powder

2 chicken thighs, deboned
Corn flour, as required

Directions:

In a bowl, mix together shallots, soy sauce and white pepper.

Add chicken thighs and coat with marinade generously.

Refrigerate to marinade for about 2-3 hours.

Remove the chicken thighs from marinade and coat with corn flour.

Preheat the Airfryer to 390 degrees F.

Arrange the chicken thighs in the Airfryer pan, with skin side down.

Cook for about 10 minutes.

Now, set the Airfryer to 355 degrees F.
Cook for about 10 minutes.

CHICKEN THIGHS WITH CHILI SAUCE

Time: 15 minutes   Servings: 2

Ingredients:

For Chicken:

1 scallion, chopped finely
1 garlic clove, minced
½ tablespoon soy sauce
½ tablespoon rice vinegar
½ teaspoon sugar
Freshly ground black pepper, to taste
2 chicken thighs, deboned

Potato flour, ad required

For Chili Sauce:

2 bird's eye chilies, chopped
1 shallots, sliced thinly
1½ tablespoon Thai chili sauce
1 tablespoon sugar
1 tablespoon fresh lime juice
Salt to taste

Directions:

For chicken in a bowl, mix together all ingredients except chicken and potato flour.
Add chicken thighs and coat with marinade generously.
Remove the chicken thighs from marinade and coat with corn flour.
Remove the chicken thighs from marinade and coat with corn flour.
Preheat the Airfryer to 390 degrees F.
Arrange the chicken thighs in the Airfryer pan, with skin side down.
Cook for about 10 minutes.
Now, set the Airfryer to 355 degrees F.
Cook for about 10 minutes.
Meanwhile for sauce in a bowl, mix together all ingredients.
Remove chicken thighs from the Airfryer and immediately, top with the sauce and serve.

CHICKEN THIGHS WITH APPLE

Time: 40 minutes   Servings: 2

Ingredients:

1 shallot, sliced thinly
1 tablespoon fresh ginger, grated finely
1 teaspoon fresh thyme, minced
½ cup apple cider
2 tablespoons maple syrup

Salt and freshly ground black pepper, to taste
2 skinless, boneless chicken thighs, cut into chunks
1 large apple, cored and cubed

Directions:

In a large bowl, mix together all ingredients except chicken and apple.
Add chicken pieces and coat with marinade generously.

Refrigerate to marinate for about 6-8 hours.

Preheat the Airfryer to 390 degrees F.

Place the chicken pieces and cubed apple in Airfryer basket.

Cook for about 20 minutes, flipping once in the middle way.

Spiced Chicken

Time: 35 minutes   Servings: 3

Ingredients:

3 chicken legs and 3 chicken thighs with skin
1 cup whole buttermilk
2 cups white flour
1 tablespoon garlic powder

1 tablespoon paprika
1 teaspoon onion powder
1 teaspoon ground cumin
½ teaspoon poultry seasoning
1 tablespoon olive oil

Directions:

In a bowl, soak chicken in buttermilk and refrigerate for about 2 hours.

In a bowl, mix together flour and seasonings

Dip chicken into flour mixture, then in buttermilk, and then in flour mixture again.

Preheat the Airfryer to 360 degrees F.

Arrange the chicken into Airfryer basket and drizzle with olive oil

Cook for about 20-25 minutes

Bacon Wrapped Chicken Breast

Time: 40 minutes   Servings: 2

Ingredients:

1 tablespoon palm sugar
6-7 Fresh basil leaves
2 tablespoons fish sauce
2 tablespoons water
2 whole chicken breasts, cut each breast in half horizontally

Salt and freshly ground black pepper, to taste
12 bacon strips
1 teaspoon honey

Directions:

In a small heavy-bottomed pan, add palm sugar on medium-low heat and cook, stirring continuously for about 2-3 minutes or till caramelized.

Stir in fish sauce, basil and water.

Remove from heat and transfer into a large bowl.

Sprinkle the chicken with salt and black pepper.

Add chicken pieces in sugar mixture and coat generously.

Refrigerate to marinate for about 4-6 hours.

Preheat the Airfryer to 365 degrees F.

Wrap each chicken piece with 3 bacon strips.

Coat each piece with honey slightly.

Place the chicken in Airfryer.

Cook for about 20 minutes, flipping once after 15 minutes.

SPINACH STUFFED CHICKEN BREAST

Time: 15 minutes   Servings: 2

Ingredients:

1 tablespoon olive oil
1¾-ounce fresh spinach
¼ cup ricotta cheese, shredded
2 chicken breasts

Salt and freshly ground black pepper, to taste
2 tablespoons cheddar cheese, grated
¼ teaspoon paprika

Directions:

In a skillet, heat oil on medium heat.

Add spinach and cook for about 3-4 minutes.

Stir in the ricotta and cook for about 30-60 seconds.

Remove from heat and keep aside to cool.

Cut slits into the chicken breasts about ¼-inch apart but not all the way through.

Stuff each chicken breast with spinach mixture.

Season the chicken breasts with salt and pepper.

Sprinkle with cheddar cheese and paprika.

Preheat the Airfryer to 390 degrees F.

Cook for about 20-25 minutes.

CHICKEN PARCEL

Time: 40 minutes   Servings: 2

Ingredients:

1 carrot, peeled and slice thinly
Salt and freshly ground black pepper, to taste
2 tablespoons butter

2 chicken breast halves
1 tablespoon fresh rosemary, chopped
1 lemon, halved

Directions:

Arrange 2 square shaped parchment papers n smooth surface.

Place carrot slices in the centre of each parchment paper evenly.

Place ½ tablespoon of butter over carrot slices in each parcel and sprinkle with salt and black pepper.

Arrange 1 chicken breast over carrot slices in each parcel.

Top each chicken breast with rosemary evenly and drizzle with lemon juice.

Top with remaining butter.

Seal each parchment paper by folding all four corners.

Preheat the Airfryer to 375 degrees F.
Arrange the chicken parcels in the Airfryer pan.
Cook for about 20-25 minutes.

CHEESE STUFFED CHICKEN BREAST

Time: 25 minutes   Servings: 2

Ingredients:

2 (8-ounce) skinless, boneless chicken
fillets
Salt and freshly ground black pepper, to
taste

4 brie cheese slices
1 tablespoon chive, minced
4 cured ham slices

Directions:

Cut each chicken fillet in 2 equal pieces.
Carefully, make a slit in each chicken piece horizontally about ¼-inch from the edge.
Open each chicken piece and season with the salt and black pepper.
Place 1 cheese slice in the open area of each chicken piece and sprinkle with chives.
Close the chicken pieces and wrap each one with a ham slice.
Preheat the Airfryer at 355 degrees F.
Place the chicken pieces in an Airfryer basket.
Cook for about 15 minutes.

SAUSAGE STUFFED CHICKEN BREAST

Time: 25 minutes   Servings: 4

Ingredients:

4 (4-ounce) skinless, boneless chicken breasts
4 sausages, casing removed

Directions:

With a rolling pin, roll each chicken breast for about 1 minute. Place 1 sausages over each chicken breast.
Roll each breast around the sausage and secure with toothpicks.
Preheat the Airfryer to 375 degrees F. Place the chicken in an Airfryer basket.
Cook for about 15 minutes.

CRISPY STUFFED CHICKEN BREAST

Time: 60 minutes   Servings: 2

Ingredients:

1 medium eggplant, halved lengthwise
Salt, to taste
Freshly ground black pepper, to taste

¼ cup pomegranate seeds
2 (4-ounce) skinless, boneless chicken
breasts

1 egg white
¼ cup plain flour
¼ cup breadcrumbs

1 tablespoon fresh thyme, chopped
½ tablespoon olive oil

Directions:

In a colander, place the eggplant halves and sprinkle with some salt.
Keep aside for about 20 minutes.
With a paper towel, dry the eggplant halves.
Preheat the Airfryer to 390 degrees F.
Place the eggplant halves in Airfryer basket, cut side up.
Cook for about 20 minutes.
Remove the eggplant from Airfryer and keep aside to cool.
With a spoon, scoop out the flesh from each eggplant half.
In a food processor, add eggplant pulp and a pinch of salt and black pepper and pulse till a puree forms.
Transfer the eggplant puree into a bowl.
Add pomegranate seeds and mix.
Carefully, cut the chicken breasts lengthwise to make a pocket.
Stuff the chicken pockets with eggplant mixture.
In a shallow dish, place the flour.
In a second shallow dish, add the egg white and a pinch of salt and black pepper and beat.
In a third shallow dish, mix together breadcrumbs, thyme and oil.
Now, preheat the Airfryer to 355 degrees F.
Coat the chicken breasts with flour.
Now, coat the chicken breasts with egg white mixture.
Sprinkle the breasts with breadcrumbs mixture generously and press to spread evenly.
Place the chicken breasts in Airfryer and cook for about 25 minutes.

Cheesy Chicken Cutlets

Time: 40 minutes

Servings: 2

Ingredients:

¾ cup all-purpose flour
2 large eggs
1½ cups (Japanese breadcrumbs) (panko)
¼ cup Parmesan cheese, grated
1 tablespoon mustard powder

Salt and freshly ground black pepper, to taste
4 (6-ounce) (¼-inch thick) skinless, boneless chicken cutlets
1 tablespoon olive oil
1 lemon, halved

Directions:

In a shallow bowl, place the flour.
In a second shallow bowl, beat the eggs.
In a third shallow bowl, mix together panko, mustard powder cheese, oil, salt and pepper.
Season chicken with, salt and black pepper
Coat the chicken in flour and shake off any excess.

Now, dip chicken in egg and then coat with panko mixture.

Preheat the Airfryer to 355 degrees F.

Arrange the chicken pieces in Airfryer.

Cook for about 30 minutes.

Spicy Chicken with Coconut

Time: 25 minutes

Servings: 4

Ingredients:

For Chicken:

½ cup coconut cream
1 garlic clove, minced
1 teaspoon fresh lime zest, grated finely
3 teaspoons avocado oil
2 tablespoons fresh lime juice
2 teaspoons soy sauce
2 teaspoons pure maple syrup

¼ teaspoon chile paste
2 teaspoons curry powder
1½ teaspoons ground coriander
1 teaspoon ground cumin
¼ teaspoons dried cilantro, crushed
Pinch of cayenne pepper
4 (4-ounce) skinless, boneless chicken breasts

Directions:

For chicken in a large bowl, add all ingredients except chicken and mix till well combined.

Add chicken and coat with marinade generously.

Cover and refrigerate to marinate for overnight.

Preheat the air fryer at 370 degrees F.

Place the chicken in an Airfryer basket in a single layer.

Cook for about 10-15 minutes.

Mongolian Chicken

Time: 35 minutes

Servings: 4

Ingredients:

1 pound boneless chicken, cubed
1 tablespoon light soy sauce
½ tablespoon corn starch
1 egg
2 tablespoons olive oil
1 medium yellow onion, sliced thinly
1 green chili, chopped
3 teaspoons garlic, minced

1 teaspoon fresh ginger, grated
5 curry leaves
½ teaspoon curry powder
1 tablespoon chili sauce
1 teaspoon sugar
½ teaspoon salt
Pinch of black pepper
½ cup evaporated milk

Directions:

In a bowl, mix together chicken, egg, soy sauce and corn starch.

Cover and leave for 1 hour. Remove and dry with paper towels.

Preheat the Airfryer to 390 degrees F.

Place the chicken in an Airfryer basket
Cook for about 10 minutes.
In a skillet, heat oil on medium heat.
Add onion, green chili, garlic and ginger and sauté for about 2 minutes.
Add chicken, curry powder, chili sauce, sugar, salt and pepper and mix till well combined.
Add evaporated milk and cook for about 3-4 minutes.

BREADED CHICKEN WITH PASTA SAUCE

Time: 45 minutes

Servings: 2

Ingredients:
2 chicken breasts
1 egg, beaten
4-ounce breadcrumbs
1 tablespoon fresh basil

2 tablespoons vegetable oil
¼ cup pasta sauce
¼ cup Parmesan cheese, grated

Directions:
Slice the chicken breast in half long way so that you have two flat pieces.
In a shallow bowl, beat the egg.
In another shallow bowl, add oil, breadcrumbs and basil and mix till a crumbly mixture forms.
Dip the chicken pieces into the beaten egg and then coat it with the breadcrumb mix.
Preheat the air fryer to 350 degrees F.
Place the chicken pieces in the air fryer.
Cook for about 15 minutes.
Spoon the pasta sauce over chicken pieces evenly sprinkle with cheese.
Cook for about 5-7 minutes more.

SPICY WHOLE CHICKEN

Time: 75 minutes

Servings: 4

Ingredients:
1 teaspoon ground cumin
½ teaspoon red pepper flakes, crushed
½ teaspoon cayenne pepper

Salt and freshly ground black pepper, to taste
1 whole chicken
Olive oil, as required

Directions:
In a bowl, mix together all spices. Coat the chicken with oil generously.
Mow, rub the chicken with spice mixture generously.
Preheat the air fryer to 350 degrees F.
Place chicken, breast side down into Airfryer.
Cook for about 30 minutes.
Flip chicken and cook for an about 30 minutes more.

LEMONY HERBED WHOLE CHICKEN

Time: 55 minutes

Servings: 4

Ingredients:

3 garlic cloves, minced
1 teaspoon fresh lemon zest, grated finely
1 teaspoon dried thyme, crushed
1 teaspoon dried oregano, crushed
1 teaspoon dried rosemary, crushed
1 teaspoon smoked paprika

Salt and freshly ground black pepper, to taste
2 tablespoons fresh lemon juice
2 tablespoons olive oil
1 (5-pound chicken)

Directions:

In a bowl, mix together all ingredients except chicken. Rub chicken with herb mixture evenly.

Keep aside in the room temperature for about 12 hour.

Preheat the Airfryer to 360 degrees F. Place chicken, breast side down into Airfryer.

Cook for about 20 minutes.

Flip chicken and cook for an about 20-25 minutes more.

WHOLE CHICKEN WITH POTATOES

Time: 70 minutes

Servings: 4

Ingredients:

1 (1½ pound) whole chicken
Salt and freshly ground black pepper, to taste

1 tablespoon olive oil, scrubbed
1 pound small potatoes

Directions:

Preheat the Airfryer to 390 degrees F.

Season the chicken with salt and black pepper.

Place the chicken in an Airfryer basket.

Cook for about 33-40 minutes.

Transfer the chicken in a plate and cover with a foil paper to keep warm.

In a bowl, add potato, oil, salt and black pepper and toss to coat well.

Place the potatoes into an Airfryer basket.

Cook for 20 minutes.

WHOLE SPRING CHICKEN

Time: 45 minutes

Servings: 3

Ingredients:

2 teaspoons dried rosemary, crushed
2 teaspoons oyster sauce

Salt and freshly ground black pepper, to taste

1 (1½-pound) spring chicken
2 bay leaves

4 bell peppers, seeded and cut into chunks
1 tablespoon olive oil

Directions:

In a bowl, mix together rosemary, oyster sauce, salt and black pepper.

Rub the chicken with rosemary mixture evenly.

Stuff the cavity of chicken with bay leaves.

Preheat the Airfryer to 360 degrees F.

Place the potatoes into an Airfryer grill pan.

Cook for 15 minutes.

Meanwhile, coat the bell pepper pieces with oil.

Remove the frill pan from Airfryer.

Transfer the chicken onto a plate.

Line the grill pan with bell pepper pieces.

Arrange chicken over bell pepper pieces.

Cook for 15 minutes more.

CORNISH GAME HEN

Time: 35 minutes

Servings: 4

Ingredients:

½ cup olive oil
1 teaspoon fresh rosemary, chopped
1 teaspoon fresh thyme, chopped
1 teaspoon fresh lemon zest, grated finely
¼ teaspoon sugar

¼ teaspoon red pepper flakes, crushed
Salt and freshly ground black pepper, to taste
2 pounds Cornish game hen, back bone removed and halved

Directions:

In a large bowl, mix together all ingredients except hen portions.

Add hen portions and coat with marinade generously.

Cover and refrigerator for about 2-24 hours.

In a strainer, place the hen portions to drain any liquid.

Preheat the Airfryer to 390 degrees F.

Place the hen portions in an Airfryer basket.

Cook for about 14-16 minutes.

SIMPLE TURKEY BREAST

Time: 50 minutes

Servings: 6

Ingredients:

1(8-pound) bone-in turkey breast
Salt and freshly ground black pepper, to taste
2 tablespoon olive oil

Directions:

Preheat the Airfryer to 360 degrees F.

Season the turkey breast with salt and black pepper and drizzle with oil.

Place breast, skin side down in Airfryer basket.

Cook for about 20 minutes.

Flip the side and cook for abbot 20-25 minutes.

*M*APLE GLAZED TURKEY BREAST

Time: 65 minutes   Servings: 6

Ingredients:

1 teaspoon dried thyme, crushed
½ teaspoon dried sage, crushed
½ teaspoon smoked paprika
Salt and freshly ground black pepper, to taste

1 (5-pound) turkey breast
2 teaspoons olive oil
¼ cup maple syrup
2 tablespoon Dijon mustard
1 tablespoon butter, softened

Directions:

Preheat the air fryer to 350 degrees F.

In a bowl, mix together herbs, paprika, salt and black pepper.

Coat the turkey breast with oil evenly.

Rub the outside of the turkey breast with the herb mixture.

Transfer the turkey breast into the Airfryer basket.

Cook for about 25 minutes.

Flip the side and cook for about 12 minutes.

Again flip the side and cook for about 12 minutes more.

Meanwhile in a bowl, mix together the maple syrup, mustard and butter.

Coat the turkey with the glaze evenly.

Cook for about 5 minutes more.

*T*URKEY LEGS

Time: 40 minutes   Servings: 6

Ingredients:

2 garlic cloves, minced
1 tablespoon fresh rosemary, minced
1 teaspoon fresh lime zest, grated finely
2 tablespoons olive oil

1 tablespoon fresh lime juice
Salt and freshly ground black pepper, to taste
2 turkey legs

Directions:

In a large bowl, mix together all ingredients except turkey legs.

Add turkey legs and coat with marinade generously.

Refrigerate to marinate for about 6-8 hours.

Preheat the air fryer to 350 degrees F.

Arrange the turkey legs in Airfryer.

Cook for about 30 minutes, flipping once in the middle way.

Beer Coated Duck Breast

Time: 35 minutes

Servings: 2

Ingredients:

For Duck Breast:
1 tablespoon olive oil
1 teaspoon mustard
1 tablespoon fresh thyme, chopped
1 cup beer
Salt and freshly ground black pepper, to taste

1 (10½-ounce) duck breast
4 cherry tomatoes
For Serving:
1 tablespoon balsamic vinegar
¼ cup black olives

Directions:

In a bowl, mix together oil, mustard, thyme, beer, salt and black pepper.

Add duck breast ad cost with marinade generously.

Refrigerate, covered for about 4 hours.

Preheat the Airfryer to 390 degrees F.

Cover the duck breast with a piece of foil.

Place the duck breast in an Airfryer basket

Cook for about 15 minutes.

Remove the foil paper from the breast.

Now, set the Airfryer to 355 degrees F.

Add tomatoes in the Airfryer basket.

Cook for about 5 minutes.

Drizzle with vinegar and serve alongside the olives.

Honey-Mustard Glazed Duck Breast

Time: 30 minutes

Servings: 2

Ingredients:

1 whole smoked duck breast
1 tablespoon honey wholegrain mustard
1 teaspoon honey

1 teaspoon tomato paste
½ teaspoon apple cider vinegar

Directions:

Preheat the Airfryer to 365 degrees F.

Place the duck breast in Airfryer basket, skin side up.

Cook for about 15 minutes.

Meanwhile in a bowl, mix together remaining ingredients.

Remove the duck breast from Airfryer and coat with the honey mixture evenly.

Now, set the Airfryer to 355 degrees F.

Cook the dusk breast for about 5 minutes more.

HERBED DUCK LEGS

Time: 40 minutes   Servings: 2

Ingredients:

1 garlic clove, minced   1 teaspoon five spice powder
½ tablespoon fresh thyme, chopped   Salt and freshly ground black pepper, to
½ tablespoon fresh parsley, chopped   taste
2 duck legs

Directions:

Preheat the Airfryer to 340 degrees F.

In a bowl, mix together garlic, herbs, five spice powder, salt and black pepper.

Rub the duck legs with garlic mixture generously.

Cook the duck legs in Airfryer for about 25 minutes.

Now, set the Airfryer to 390 degrees F.

Cook for about 5 minutes more.

LAMB WITH POTATOES

Time: 40 minutes   Servings: 4

Ingredients:

1 pounds 5 ounce lamb rump   ½ of large onion, peeled and halved
2 garlic clove, crushed   2 teaspoons olive oil
1 tablespoon dried rosemary, crushed   ¼ cup frozen sweet potato fries
3 medium potatoes, peeled and halved

Directions:

Preheat the Airfryer to 355 degrees F.

Rub the lamb with crushed garlic evenly.

Sprinkle with rosemary evenly.

Arrange a divider in Airfryer.

Place the lamb in in one side of Airfryer divider. Cook for about 20 minutes.

Meanwhile in a microwave safe bowl, place the potatoes and microwave for about 4 minutes.

Drain the water from the potatoes.

In a large bowl, add potato, onions and oil and toss to coat well.

After 20 minutes set the Airfryer to 390 degrees F.

Change the side of lamb ramp and top with potato and onion halves.

In another part of Airfryer divider, place the sweet potato fries.

Cook for about 15 minutes, flipping the vegetable once after 10 minutes.

GARLICKY LAMB CHOPS

Time: 45 minutes   Servings: 4

Ingredients:

¼ cup olive oil, divided
1 bulb garlic
1 tablespoon fresh oregano, chopped
1 tablespoon fresh thyme, chopped

Salt and freshly ground black pepper, to taste
8 (4-ounce) lamb chops

Directions:

Preheat the Airfryer to 390 degrees F.
Coat the garlic bulb with about 2 tablespoons of the olive oil.
Place the garlic bulb in an Airfryer basket.
Cook for about 12 minutes.
In a large bowl, mix together remaining oil, herbs, salt and black pepper.
Coat the chops with about 1 tablespoon of the herb mixture.
Place 4 chops in Airfryer basket with garlic bulb.
Cook for about 5 minutes.
Repeat with the remaining lamb chops.
Squeeze the garlic bulb in remaining herb mixture and mix till well combined.
Serve lamb chops with herb mixture.

LAMB CHOPS WITH VEGGIES

Time: 30 minutes   Servings: 4

Ingredients:

2 tablespoons fresh rosemary, minced
2 tablespoons fresh mint leaves, minced
1 garlic clove, minced
3 tablespoons olive oil
Salt and freshly ground black pepper, to taste

4 (6-ounce) lamb chops
1 purple carrot, peeled and cubed
1 yellow carrot, peeled and cubed
1 parsnip, peeled and cubed
1 fennel bulb, cubed

Directions:

In a large bowl, mix together herbs, garlic and oil. Add chops and coat with mixture generously.
Refrigerate to marinate for about 3 hours. In a large pan of water, soak the vegetables for about 15 minutes.
Drain the vegetables completely.
Preheat the Airfryer to 390 degrees F.
Place the chops in an Airfryer basket.
Cook for about 2 minutes.
Remove the chops from the Airfryer.
Place the vegetables in the Airfryer basket and top with the chops.
Cook for about 6 minutes.

ALMONDS CRUSTED RACK OF LAMB

Time: 50 minutes

Servings: 6

Ingredients:

1 tablespoon olive oil
1 garlic clove, minced
Salt and freshly ground black pepper, to taste
1¾ pound rack of lamb

1 egg
1 tablespoon breadcrumbs
3-ounce almonds, chopped finely
1 tablespoon fresh rosemary, chopped

Directions:

In a bowl, mix together oil, garlic, salt and black pepper. Coat the rack of lamb with oil mixture evenly.
In a shallow dish, beat the egg. In another shallow dish mix together breadcrumbs, almonds and rosemary.
Dip the rack of lamb in egg and then coat with almond mixture.
Preheat the Airfryer to 220 degrees F.
Place the rack of lamb in an Airfryer basket.
Cook for about 30 minutes.
Now, set the Airfryer to 390 degrees F.
Cook for about 5 minutes more.

LEG OF LAMB

Time: 85 minutes

Servings: 4

Ingredients:

2 pound 3 ounce leg of lamb
2 tablespoons olive oil
Salt and freshly ground black pepper, to taste

2 fresh rosemary sprigs
2 fresh thyme sprigs

Directions:

Preheat the Airfryer to 300 degrees F.
Coat the leg of lamb with oil and sprinkle with salt and black pepper.
Wrap the leg of lamb with herb sprigs.
Place the chops in an Airfryer basket.
Cook for about 75 minutes.

SIMPLE STEAK

Time: 20 minutes

Servings: 2

Ingredients:

½ pound quality cuts steak
Salt and freshly ground black pepper, to taste

Directions:

Preheat the Airfryer to 390 degrees F.
Rub the steak with salt and pepper evenly.
Place the steak in air fryer basket.
Cook for about 14 minutes crispy.

Rib Rye Steak

Time: 25 minutes   Servings: 4

Ingredients:

2 pounds rib eye steak   1 tablespoon steak rub
1 tablespoon olive oil

Directions:

Preheat the Airfryer to 400 degrees F.
Drizzle the steak with olive oil and rub with seasoning generously.
Place the steak in air fryer basket.
Cook for about 14 minutes crispy.

Spicy Skirt Steak

Time: 25 minutes   Servings: 4

Ingredients:

3 garlic cloves, minced   1 teaspoon cayenne pepper
1 cup fresh parsley leaves, chopped finely   1 teaspoon red pepper flakes, crushed
3 tablespoons fresh oregano, chopped   Salt and freshly ground black pepper, to
finely   taste
3 tablespoons fresh mint leaves, chopped   ¾ cup olive oil
finely   3 tablespoons red wine vinegar
1 tablespoon ground cumin   2 (8-ounce) skirt steaks
2 teaspoons smoked paprika

Directions:

In a bowl, mix together all ingredients except the steaks.
In a reseal able bag, add ¼ cup of the herb mixture and steaks and shake to coat well.
Refrigerate for about 24 hours.
Reserve the remaining herb mixture.
Remove steaks from the refrigerator and keep in the room temperature for about 30 minutes.
Preheat the Airfryer to 390 degrees F.
Place the steaks in an Airfryer basket.
Cook for about 8-10 minutes.
Top with remaining herb mixture and serve.

Spicy Sirloin Steak

Time: 20 minutes

Servings: 2

Ingredients:
1 cup white flour
2 eggs
1 cup panko
1 teaspoon garlic powder

1 teaspoon onion powder
Salt and freshly ground black pepper, to taste
2 (6-ounce) sirloin steaks, pounded

Directions:
In a shallow bowl, place the flour. In a second shallow bowl, beat the eggs.
In a third shallow bowl, mix together panko and spices.
Coat the steak in flour, then egg, and finally panko mixture.
Place the steaks in Airfryer basket.
Preheat the Airfryer to 360 degrees F.
Cook for about 10 minutes.

Steak with Veggies

Time: 35 minutes

Servings: 4

Ingredients:
¼ cup olive oil, divided
2 tablespoons soy sauce
2 tablespoons honey
1 (12-ounce) skirt steaks, cut into thin strips

½ pound fresh mushrooms, quartered
6-ounce snow peas
1 onion, cut into half rings
Salt and freshly ground black pepper, to taste

Directions:
In a bowl, mix together 2 tablespoons of oil, soy sauce and honey.
Add steak strips and coat with mixture generously.
In another bowl, add vegetables, remaining oil, salt and black pepper and toss to coat well.
Preheat the Airfryer to 390 degrees F.
Place the steak strips and vegetables in an Airfryer basket.
Cook for about 5 minutes.

Beef Roast

Time: 40 minutes

Servings: 3

Ingredients:
2 pound 3¼-ounce topside of beef
1 tablespoon cayenne pepper

Salt and freshly ground black pepper, to taste
1 tablespoon olive oil

Directions:

Coat the beef with cayenne pepper, salt, black pepper and oil evenly.

Keep aside for about 15-20 minutes.

Preheat the Airfryer to 400 degrees F.

Cook for about 10 minutes.

Now, set the Airfryer at 375 degrees F.

Cook for about 20 minutes.

𝒫ORK SPARE RIBS

Time: 30 minutes   Servings: 4

Ingredients:

5-6 garlic cloves, minced   12 (1-inch) pork spare ribs
½ cup rice vinegar   Cornstarch, as required
2 tablespoons soy sauce   2 tablespoons olive oil
Salt and freshly ground black pepper, to
taste

Directions:

In a large bowl, mix together garlic, vinegar, soy sauce, salt and black pepper.

Add ribs and coat with mixture generously.

Refrigerate to marinate for overnight.

In a shallow bowl, add cornstarch.

Coat the ribs with cornstarch.

Drizzle with oil evenly.

Preheat the Airfryer to 390 degrees F.

Place the ribs in Airfryer basket.

Cook for about 10minutes per side.

𝓑ARBECUE FLAVORED PORK RIBS

Time: 25 minutes   Servings: 6

Ingredients:

¼ cup honey, divided   1 tablespoon soy sauce
¾ cup BBQ sauce   ½ teaspoon garlic powder
2 tablespoons tomato ketchup   Freshly ground white pepper, to taste
1 tablespoon Worcestershire sauce   1¾ pound pork ribs

Directions:

In a large bowl, mix together 3 tablespoons of honey and remaining ingredients except pork ribs.

Refrigerate to marinate for about 20 minutes.

Preheat the Airfryer to 355 degrees F.

Place the ribs in an Airfryer basket.

Cook for about 13 minutes.
Remove the ribs from Airfryer and coat with remaining honey.
Serve hot.

CARAMELIZED PORK SHOULDER

Time: 30 minutes   Servings: 8

Ingredients:

1/3 cup soy sauce
2 tablespoons sugar
1 tablespoon honey

2 pound pork shoulder, cut into 1½-inch thick slices

Directions:

In a bowl, mix together all ingredients except pork.
Add pork and coat with marinade generously.
Cover and refrigerate o marinate for about 2-8 hours.
Preheat the Airfryer to 335 degrees F.
Place the pork in an Airfryer basket.
Cook for about 10 minutes.
Now, set the Airfryer to 390 degrees F.
Cook for about 5-7 minutes more.

SWEET & SOUR PORK SHOULDER

Time: 45 minutes   Servings: 4

Ingredients:

For Pork:

10 ½-ouncepork shoulder, cut into bite sized pieces
2 pinches of Maggi seasoning
1 teaspoon light soy sauce
Dash of sesame oil
1 egg
Plain flour, as required

For Sauce:

1 teaspoon olive oil
1 medium onion, sliced
1 tablespoon garlic, minced
1 large pineapple slice, cubed
1 medium tomato, chopped
2 tablespoons tomato sauce
2 tablespoons oyster sauce
1 tablespoon Worcestershire sauce
Sugar, to taste
1 tablespoon water
½ tablespoon corn flour

Directions:

In a bowl, mix together pork cubes, Maggi seasoning, soy sauce and sesame oil.
Refrigerate to marinate for about 4-6 hours.
In a shallow dish, beat the egg.

In another shallow dish, place the plain flour.

Dip the cubed pork in egg and then coat with flour evenly.

Preheat the Airfryer to 248 degrees F.

Place the pork in Airfryer.

Cook for about 20 minutes.

For sauce in a skillet, heat oil on medium heat.

Add garlic and sauté for about 2-3 minutes.

Add pineapple and tomato and cook for about 1 minute.

Stir in tomato sauce, oyster sauce, Worcestershire sauce and sugar.

Meanwhile in a small bowl, mix together water and corn flour.

Add the corn flour mixture in the sauce, stirring continuously.

Cook, stirring continuously till sauce becomes thick.

Remove the park from Airfryer and add in the sauce.

Cook for about 1-2 minutes or till coated completely.

*B*READED PORK CHOPS

Time: 25 minutes   Servings: 2

Ingredients:
2 pork chops
Salt and freshly ground black pepper, to taste
1 egg

¼ cup plain flour
4-ounce breadcrumbs
1 tablespoon vegetable oil

Directions:
Season the pork chop with salt and pepper evenly.

In a shallow bowl, place flour

In a second shallow bowl, beat the egg.

In a third shallow bowl, add the breadcrumbs and oil and mix till a crumbly mixture forms.

Coat the pork chop in the flour, then the eggs and finally with the breadcrumbs mixture evenly.

Preheat the Airfryer to 400 degrees F.

Place the chops in Airfryer basket.

Cook for about 10 minutes.

Flip the side and cook for about 5 minutes more.

*S*WEET & SOUR PORK CHOPS

Time: 30 minutes   Servings: 4

Ingredients:
6 pork loin chops
Salt and freshly ground black pepper, to taste
2 garlic cloves, minced

2 tablespoons honey
2 tablespoons soy sauce
1 tablespoon balsamic vinegar
¼ teaspoon ground ginger

Directions:

With a meat tenderizer, tenderize the chops completely.

Sprinkle the chops with a little salt and black pepper.

In a large bowl, mix together remaining ingredients.

Add chops and coat with marinade generously.

Refrigerate, covered for about 2-8 hours.

Preheat the Airfryer to 355 degrees F.

Place the chops in a baking tray and cook for about 5-8 minutes from both sides.

PORK CHOPS WITH PEANUT SAUCE

Time: 30 minutes   Servings: 4

Ingredients:

For Pork:
1 teaspoon fresh ginger, minced
1 garlic clove, minced
2 tablespoon soy sauce
1 tablespoon olive oil
1 teaspoon hot pepper sauce
1 pound pork chops, cubed into 1-inch size
For Peanut Sauce:

1 tablespoon olive oil
1 shallot, chopped finely
1 garlic clove, minced
1 teaspoon ground coriander
¾ cup ground peanuts
1 tablespoon olive oil
1 teaspoon hot pepper sauce
¾ cup coconut milk

Directions:

For pork in a bowl, mix together all ingredients.

Keep aside for about 15 minutes. Preheat the Airfryer at 390 degrees F.

Place the pork in an Airfryer basket.

Cook for about 12 minutes.

Meanwhile for sauce in a pan, heat oil on medium heat.

Add shallot and garlic and sauté for about 2-3 minutes.

Add coriander and sauté for about 1 minute.

Stir in remaining ingredients and cook, stirring continuously for about 5 minutes.

In serving plates, place pork.

Top with sauce and serve.

HERBED PORK CHOPS WITH SALSA

Time: 75 minutes   Servings: 2

Ingredients:

2 (1-inch thick) pork chops
2 garlic cloves, minced
½ tablespoon fresh cilantro, chopped
½ tablespoon fresh rosemary, chopped
½ tablespoon fresh parsley, chopped

2 tablespoons olive oil
¾ tablespoon Dijon mustard
1 tablespoon ground coriander
1 teaspoon sugar
Salt, to taste

Directions:

For chops in a bowl, mix together all ingredients except the chops.

Add pork chops and coat with marinade generously.

Cover and refrigerator for about 2-3 hours.

Remove chops from the refrigerator and keep in room temperature for about 30 minutes.

Preheat the Airfryer to 390 degrees F.

Place the chops in an Airfryer basket.

Cook for about 10-12 minutes.

PORK LOIN WITH POTATOES

Time: 40 minutes   Servings: 2

Ingredients:

2 pounds pork loin
1 teaspoon fresh parsley, chopped
2 large red potatoes, chopped
½ teaspoon garlic powder

½ teaspoon red pepper flakes, crushed
Salt and freshly ground black pepper, to taste

Directions:

In a large bowl, add all ingredients except glaze and toss to coat well.

Preheat the Airfryer to 325 degrees F.

Place the loin in an Airfryer basket.

Arrange the potatoes around pork loin.

Cook for about 25 minutes.

PORK TENDERLOIN WITH BELL PEPPER

Time: 30 minutes   Servings: 2

Ingredients:

1 red bell pepper, seeded and cut into thin strips
1 red onion, sliced thinly
2 teaspoon Herbs de Provence
Salt and freshly ground black pepper, to taste

1 tablespoon olive oil
10½-ounce pork tenderloin, cut into 4 pieces
½ tablespoon mustard

Directions:

In a bowl, mix together bell pepper, onion, Herbs de Provence, salt, black pepper and ½ tablespoon of oil.

Rub the pork pieces with mustard, salt and black pepper.

Drizzle with oil. Transfer the bell pepper mixture into Airfryer pan.

Top with the pork pieces.

Preheat the Airfryer to 390 degrees F,

Cook for about 15 minutes, turning once in the middle way.

Pork Tenderloin with Veggies

Time: 40 minutes   Servings: 2

Ingredients:

4 potatoes   2 pork tenderloins
¾ pound frozen green beans   1 tablespoon olive oil
6 bacon slices

Directions:

Preheat the Airfryer to 390 degrees F.
With a fork, pierce the potatoes.
Place the potatoes in the Airfryer.
Cook for about 15 minutes.
Wrap the green beans with bacon slices.
Coat the pork tenderloin with some oil
After 15 minutes, add pork tenderloin in Airfryer with potatoes and cook for about 5 minutes.
After 5 minutes, remove the pork tenderloin.
Place the bean rolls in the basket and top with the pork tenderloin.
Cook for about 7 minutes.

Pork Neck with Salad

Time: 40 minutes   Servings: 2

Ingredients:

For Pork: 1 bunch fresh basil leaves
                                                           1 bunch fresh cilantro leaves
1 tablespoon soy sauce
1 tablespoon fish sauce   **For Dressing:**
½ tablespoon oyster sauce   3 tablespoons fish sauce
½ pound pork neck   2 tablespoons olive oil
For Salad: 1 teaspoon apple cider vinegar
1 ripe tomato, sliced tickly   1 tablespoon palm sugar
8-10 Thai shallots, sliced   2 bird eye chili
1 scallion, chopped   1 tablespoon garlic, minced

Directions:

For pork in a bowl, mix together all ingredients except pork.
Add pork neck and coat with marinade evenly.
Refrigerate for about 2-3 hours.
Preheat the Airfryer to 340 degrees F.
Place the pork neck onto a grill pan.
Cook for about 12 minutes.
Meanwhile in a large salad bowl, mix together all salad ingredients.

In a bowl, add all dressing ingredients and beat till well combined.

Remove pork neck from Airfryer and cut into desired slices.

Place pork slices over salad.

Add dressing and toss to coat well.

GLAZED HAM

Time: 50 minutes   Servings: 4

Ingredients:

1 pound 10½ ounce ham joint   2 tablespoons French mustard
¾ cup whiskey   2 tablespoons honey

Directions:

Keep ham joint in room temperature for about 30 minutes before cooking.

In a bowl, mix together remaining ingredients.

In a baking dish, place the ham.

Top with half of honey mixture and coat over ham evenly.

Preheat the Airfryer to 320 degrees F.

Cook for about 15 minutes.

Flip the side of ham and top with remaining honey mixture.

Cook for about 25 minutes.

SAUSAGE WITH VEGGIES

Time: 55 minutes   Servings: 2

Ingredients:

4 pork sausages   14-ounce butterbeans, drained and rinsed
1 bell pepper, seeded and chopped   1 (14-ounce) can chopped tomatoes
2 zucchinis, chopped   2 fresh thyme sprigs
1 eggplant, chopped   1 tablespoon balsamic vinegar
1 medium red onion, chopped   2 garlic cloves
1 tablespoon vegetable oil   1 chili

Directions:

Preheat the Airfryer to 400 degrees F.

Place the vegetables in the Airfryer and drizzle with the oil.

Cook for about 20 minutes.

Transfer the vegetables into a bowl.

Now, set the air fryer to 350 degrees F.

Place the sausage in Airfryer.

Cook for about 10-15 minutes

Meanwhile in a pan, mix together the vegetables with the remaining ingredients and bring to a simmer.

In a serving dish, place the sausage and vegetable mixture and serve.

Cajun Spiced Salmon

Time: 15 minutes

Servings: 2

Ingredients:

2 salmon steaks

2 tablespoons Cajun seasoning

Directions:

Rub the salmon with the Cajun seasoning evenly.
Keep aside for about 10 minutes.
Preheat the Airfryer to 390 degrees F.
Arrange the salmon steaks on the grill pan.
Cook for about 8 minutes, flipping once in the middle way.

Lemony Salmon

Time: 15 minutes

Servings: 2

Ingredients:

2 (7-ounce) (¾-inch thick) salmon fillets
1 tablespoon Cajun seasoning

1 tablespoon fresh lemon juice

Directions:

Preheat the air fryer to 355 degrees F.
Sprinkle the salmon with Cajun seasoning evenly.
Place the fish in an Airfryer, grill pan, skin-side up.
Cook for about 7 minutes.
Serve with the drizzling of lemon juice.

Honey Glazed Salmon

Time: 15 minutes

Servings: 2

Ingredients:

2 salmon fillets
Salt, to taste

Honey, as required

Directions:

Sprinkle the salmon fillets with salt evenly.
Coat both fillets with honey evenly.
Preheat the Airfryer at 355 degrees F.
Place the salmon fillets in Airfryer.
Cook for about 8 minutes.

Sweet & Sour Glazed Salmon

Time: 20 minutes

Servings: 2

Ingredients:

1/3 cup soy sauce
1/3 cup honey
3 teaspoons rice wine vinegar

1 teaspoon water
2 (3½-ounce) salmon fillets

Directions:

In a small bowl, mix together all ingredients except salmon.
In a small bowl, reserve about half of the mixture.
Add the salmon in remaining mixture and coat well.
Cover and refrigerate to marinate for about 2 hours.
Preheat the Airfryer to 355 degrees F.
Place the salmon in Airfryer grill pan.
Cook for about 13 minutes, flipping once after 8 minutes and coating with reserved marinade after every 3 minutes.
For sauce in a small pan, place the reserved and cook for about 1 minute.
Serve salmon with marinade sauce.

Salmon Parcel

Time: 20 minutes

Servings: 2

Ingredients:

2 salmon fillets
4 asparagus stalks
¼ cup white sauce
1 teaspoon oil

¼ cup champagne
Salt and freshly ground black pepper, to taste

Directions:

Preheat the air fryer to 355 degrees F.
In a bowl, mix together all ingredients.
Divide the salmon mixture over 2 foil papers evenly.
Seal the foil paper to form the packet.
Place the salmon packets in Airfryer basket.
Cook for about 11-13 minutes or till desired doneness.

Salmon with Pesto

Time: 40 minutes

Servings: 4

Ingredients:

For Salmon:

4 (6-ounce) salmon fillets

2 teaspoons olive oil
Pinch of salt
For Pesto:
3 cups fresh basil leaves
1½ cups cashews

4 garlic cloves, chopped
¼ cup Parmesan cheese, grated
Salt and freshly ground black pepper, to taste
1 cup olive oil

Directions:
Preheat the air fryer to 270 degrees F.

Drizzle the salmon with oil evenly and sprinkle with a pinch of salt.

Place the salmon into Airfryer basket. Cook for about 20-23 minutes.

For pesto in a food processor, add basil leaves, cashews, garlic, cheese, salt and black pepper and pulse till well combined.

While, motor is running, slowly, add the oil and pulse till smooth.

Place pesto over cooked salmon and serve.

STEAMED SALMON WITH DILL SAUCE

Time: 30 minutes

Servings: 2

Ingredients:
1 cup water
2 (6-ounce) salmon fillets
2 teaspoons olive oil
Salt, to taste

½ cup sour cream
½ cup Greek yogurt
2 tablespoons fresh dill, chopped and divided

Directions:
Preheat the Airfryer to 285 degrees F.

In the bottom of the Airfryer pan, place the water

Coat the salmon with olive oil and sprinkle with a pinch of salt.

Place the salmon in an Airfryer and cook for about 9-11 minutes.

Meanwhile, in a bowl, mix together remaining ingredients.

Serve salmon with dill sauce.

SALMON WITH ZUCCHINI NOODLES

Time: 30 minutes

Servings: 2

Ingredients:

For Salmon:
2 (5¼-ounce) skin-on salmon fillets
1 teaspoon olive oil
Salt and freshly ground black pepper, to taste
For Zucchini Noodles:
1 ripe avocado, peeled, pitted and chopped

½ of garlic clove, chopped
2 tablespoons fresh parsley
Salt and freshly ground black pepper, to taste
2 large zucchinis, spiralized with blade C
2 tablespoons pine nuts, toasted

Directions:

Preheat the Airfryer at 355 degrees F.

Coat the salmon with the oil and season with the salt and black pepper.

Place the salmon fillets in the Airfryer.

Cook for about 10 minutes.

Meanwhile in a food processor, add the avocado, garlic, parsley, salt and black pepper and pulse till smooth.

In a bowl, add the zucchini noodles and avocado sauce and toss to coat.

Divide the zucchini noodles in 2 plates and top with the salmon.

Serve with the garnishing of pine nuts.

Citrus Glazed Halibut

Time: 45 minutes   Servings: 2

Ingredients:

1 garlic clove, minced   ½ cup cooking wine
¼ teaspoon fresh ginger, grated finely   ¼ cup sugar
½ cup low-sodium soy sauce   ¼ teaspoon red pepper flakes, crushed
¼ cup fresh orange juice   1 pound haddock steak
2 tablespoons lime juice

Directions:

In a pan, add all ingredients except haddock steak and bring to a boil.

Cook, stirring continuously for about 3-4 minutes.

Remove from the heat and keep aside to cool.

In a reseal able bag, add half of marinade and haddock steak and shake to coat well.

Refrigerate for about 30 minutes.

Reserve the remaining marinade.

Preheat the Airfryer to 390 degrees F.

Place the haddock steak in an Airfryer basket.

Cook for about 9-11 minutes.

Remove from the Airfryer and immediately, coat with the remaining glaze.

Serve hot.

Haddock with Cheese Sauce

Time: 20 minutes   Servings: 2

Ingredients:

2 (6-ounce) haddock fillets   1 tablespoon Parmesan cheese, grated
1 tablespoon olive oil   ½ cup extra-virgin olive oil
Salt and freshly ground black pepper, to
taste
2 tablespoons pine nuts
3 tablespoons fresh basil, chopped

Directions:

Preheat the Airfryer at 355 degrees F.

Coat the fish fillets with oil evenly and sprinkle with salt and black pepper.

Place the fish fillets in an Airfryer basket.

Cook for about 8 minutes.

Meanwhile in a food processor, add remaining ingredients and pulse till smooth.

Transfer the fish fillets in serving plates.

Top with cheese sauce and serve.

BREADED FISH

Time: 25 minutes   Servings: 2

Ingredients:

1 egg   4 fish fillets (of your choice)
4-ounce breadcrumbs   1 lemon, cut into wedges
2 tablespoons vegetable oil

Directions:

Preheat the air fryer to 350 degrees F.

In a bowl, beat the egg.

In another bowl, add the breadcrumbs and oil and mix till a crumbly mixture forms.

Dip the fish fillets into the egg and remove any residual.

Now, coat the fish fillet with the crumb mixture.

Carefully, place the fillet in the Airfryer.

Cook for about 12 minutes.

Serve immediately with lemon wedges.

SESAME SEEDS COATED FISH

Time: 20 minutes   Servings: 5

Ingredients:

3 tablespoons plain flour   Pinch of salt
2 eggs   Pinch of black pepper
½ cup sesame seeds, toasted   3 tablespoons olive oil
½ cup breadcrumbs   5 frozen fish fillets (white fish of your
1/8 teaspoon dried rosemary, crushed   choice)

Directions:

In a shallow dish, place flour

In a second shallow dish, beat the eggs

In a third shallow dish, add remaining ingredients except fish fillets and mix till a crumbly mixture forms.

Coat the fillets with flour and shake off the excess flour.

Next, dip the fillets in egg.

Then coat the fillets with sesame seeds mixture generously.
Preheat the Airfryer to 390 degrees F.
Line an Airfryer basket with a piece of foil.
Arrange the fillets into prepared basket.
Cook for about 14 minutes, flipping once after 10 minutes.

CRUMBED COD

Time: 25 minutes   Servings: 2

Ingredients:

2 (4-ounce) skinless cod fish fillets, cut into rectangular pieces
½ cup flour
3 eggs
2 garlic cloves, minced

1 green chili, chopped finely
3 scallions, chopped finely
1 teaspoon soy sauce
Salt and freshly ground black pepper, to taste

Directions:

In a shallow dish, place the flour.
In another shallow dish, add remaining ingredients except cod and beat well.
Coat each fillet first into the flour and then dip in egg mixture.
Preheat the Airfryer to 375 degrees F.
Place the fish in an Airfryer basket
Cook for about 7 minutes.

CHINESE STYLE COD

Time: 30 minutes   Servings: 4

Ingredients:

2 (7-ounce) cod fillets
Salt and freshly ground black pepper, to taste
¼ teaspoon sesame oil
1 cup water
5 little squares rock sugar

5 tablespoons light soy sauce
1 teaspoon dark soy sauce
2 scallions, sliced (green part)
¼ cup fresh cilantro, chopped
3 tablespoons olive oil
5 ginger slices

Directions:

Season the cod fillets with salt and black pepper evenly and drizzle with sesame oil.
Keep aside in room temperature for about 15-20 minutes.
Preheat the Airfryer to 355 degrees F. Place the fish fillets in Airfryer.
Cook for about 12 minutes. Meanwhile in a small pan, add water and bring to a boil.
Add rock sugar and both soy sauces and cook, stirring continuously till sugar dissolves.
Remove from heat. Remove cod fillets from Airfryer.
Cut each fillet in 2 equal sized portions.

Divide fish fillets in 4 serving plates and top with scallion and cilantro.

In a small frying pan, heat oil on medium heat.

Add ginger slices and sauté for about 2-3 minutes.

Discard the ginger slices.

Carefully, pour hot oil over fillets evenly.

Top with sauce mixture and serve.

SHRIMP WITH RICE

Time: 35 minutes   Servings: 4

Ingredients:

For Shrimp:

1 pound tiger shrimp
3 tablespoons olive oil
1 teaspoon old bay seasoning
½ teaspoon cayenne pepper
½ teaspoon smoked paprika
Salt, to taste

For Rice:

1 tablespoon olive oil
½ cup celery stalk, chopped

½ cup onion, chopped
½ cup jalapeño peppers, chopped
Salt, to taste
1 cup tomatoes, chopped finely
1 cup long grain rice
¼ teaspoon old bay seasoning
¼ teaspoon cayenne pepper
¼ teaspoon smoked paprika
¼ teaspoon paprika
1¼ cups chicken broth

Directions:

For shrimp in a bowl, mix together all ingredients.

Cover and keep aside.

For the rice in a large pan, heat 1 tablespoon olive oil on medium heat.

Add celery, onion, jalapenos and salt and sauté for about 4-5 minutes.

Add tomatoes and cook for about 1-2 minutes.

Add rice and, spices and chicken broth and bring to a boil on high heat.

Reduced heat to low and simmer covered for about 15 minutes.

Preheat the Airfryer to 390 degrees F.

Place the shrimp in an Airfryer basket.

Cook for about 4-5 minutes.

Serve shrimp over the rice.

RICE IN CRAB SHELL

Time: 20 minutes   Servings: 2

Ingredients:

1 bowl cooked rice
4 tablespoons crab meat
2 tablespoons chopped onion

2 tablespoons spring onion
2 tablespoons butter
Paprika, to taste

2 tablespoons shredded Parmesan cheese   2 crab shells

Directions:

In a bowl, mix together rice, crab meat, onion, spring onion, butter and paprika.

Fill crab shell with rice mixture.

Top with cheese.

Preheat the air fryer at 390 degrees F.

Place the crab shell in Airfryer basket.

Cook for about 8 minutes.

Sprinkle with more paprika and serve.

Prawns with Sweet Potato

Time: 40 minutes   Servings: 4

Ingredients:

For Prawns:

1½ pound prawns, peeled and deveined
1 shallot, chopped
4 garlic cloves, minced
1 red chili pepper, seeded and chopped
2 tablespoons olive oil
½ teaspoon smoked paprika

For Sweet Potatoes:

5 large sweet potatoes, peeled and cut into slices
2 tablespoons fresh rosemary, chopped finely
2 tablespoons olive oil
1 tablespoon honey

Directions:

For prawns in a large bowl, mix together all ingredients.

Refrigerate to marinate for about 2 hours.

For sweet potato in a bowl, add all ingredients and toss to coat well.

Preheat the Airfryer to 355 degrees F.

Place the sweet potato slices in an Airfryer basket.

Cook for about 15 minutes.

Transfer the sweet potato slices in a plate.

Now, set the Airfryer to 390 degrees F.

Thread the prawns onto lemongrass stalks.

Cook for about 5 minutes.

Serve the prawns with sweet potato slices.

Honey Glazed Calamari

Time: 25 minutes   Servings: 4

Ingredients:

For Calamari:
½ pound calamari tubes, cut into ¼-inch rings

1 cup club soda
1 cup flour
½ tablespoon red pepper flakes, crushed

Salt and freshly ground black pepper, to taste

For Sauce:
2 tablespoons Sriracha

Red pepper flakes, to taste
½ cup honey
Cooking spray

Directions:

Wash calamari and cut into ¼ inch rings. Transfer the calamari into a bowl and cover with club soda. Keep aside for about 10 minutes.

Meanwhile, in a bowl, mix together flour, red pepper flakes, salt and black pepper.

Drain the club soda from the calamari.

With the paper towels, pat dry the calamari rings.

Coat the calamari rings in flour mixture evenly.

Preheat the Airfryer at 375 degrees F.

Grease the Airfryer basket.

Place the calamari rings in prepared Airfryer basket.

Cook for about 11 minutes, shaking occasionally.

Meanwhile, in a bowl, mix together Sriracha, honey and red pepper flakes.

Remove from Airfryer and coat calamari rings with Sriracha sauce.

Place the calamari rings in the Airfryer basket.

Cook for about 2 minutes.

CHEESY VEGGIES

Time: 50 minutes

Servings: 2

Ingredients:

1 onion, sliced thinly
1 tomato, sliced thinly
1 zucchini,
1 yellow squash, sliced thinly
1 teaspoon olive oil

½ cup cheddar cheese, grated
1 teaspoon mixed dried herbs
Salt and freshly ground black pepper, to taste

Directions:

Preheat the air fryer to 355 degrees F.

In a baking dish, spread the vegetables in a single layer.

Drizzle with oil and sprinkle with herbs, salt and black pepper.

Top with cheese evenly.

Cook for about 30 minutes.

VEGGIES WITH CHEESE SAUCE

Time: 20 minutes

Servings: 3

Ingredients:

1 (16-ounce) bag frozen vegetables

1 can cheese sauce

Directions:

Preheat the Airfryer to 400 degrees F.

Arrange the vegetables in an Airfryer basket.

Cook for about 10-12 minutes.

Place the vegetables in serving plate.

Cover with cheese sauce and serve.

GREEN BEANS & RICE CASSEROLE

Time: 50 minutes   Servings: 4

Ingredients:

1 cup cooked rice

25-ounce canned green beans

¼ cup cream of mushroom soup

½ cup ricotta cheese, crumbled

1 cup mozzarella cheese, grated

Pinch of salt

2 cups plain flour

2 cups breadcrumbs

2 eggs

Directions:

In a bowl, mix together the rice, green beans, soup, ricotta, mozzarella and salt.

Refrigerate for about 30 minutes.

In a shallow bowl, place the flour.

In a second shallow bowl, beat the eggs.

In a third shallow bowl, place the breadcrumbs.

Make small sized balls from the mixture.

Roll the balls in the flour, then dip in the egg.

Now, roll in the breadcrumbs evenly.

Preheat the air fryer to 380 degrees F.

Cook for about 8 minutes.

BREADED RAVIOLI

Time: 35 minutes   Servings: 6

Ingredients:

3 eggs

2 cups flour

2 cups Italian-style bread crumbs

12 pre-made frozen cheese ravioli

1 cup buttermilk

1 jar Marinara sauce

Directions:

In a shallow bowl, beat the eggs.

In a second shallow bowl, place the flour.

In a third shallow dish, place the breadcrumbs.

Dip the ravioli in eggs and then cot with flour.

Now, coat the ravioli into breadcrumbs.

Preheat the air fryer at 370 degrees F.

Place the breaded ravioli in Airfryer basket.

Cook for about 20 minutes.

Serve with marinara sauce.

$\mathcal{V}$EGGIE LASAGNA

Time: 75 minutes   Servings: 4

Ingredients:

2 tablespoons sunflower oil

1½ pound pumpkin, peeled and chopped finely

1 onion, chopped

1½ tablespoons fresh rosemary, chopped

¾ pound tomatoes, cubed

1 pound cooked beets, sliced thinly

8-ounce mild goat cheese, grated

½ pound fresh lasagna sheets

¼ cup Parmesan cheese, grated

Directions:

Preheat the Airfryer to 345 degrees F.

In a large bowl, add 1 tablespoon oil, pumpkin, onion and rosemary and toss to coat well.

Cook for about 10 minutes.

In a blender, add pumpkin mixture and tomatoesand pulse till smooth puree forms.

Transfer the puree in a skillet on low heat and cook for about 5 minutes.

Lightly grease a baking dish.

Cover the bottom of the prepared baking dish with enough pumpkin puree.

Place 1 layer of the lasagna sheets over the puree.

Place half of sauce, followed by 1/3 of the beet slices and 1/3 f the cheese.

Repeat the layers and top with the parmesan evenly.

Now, set the Airfryer to 300 degrees F.

Cook for about 45 minutes.

$\mathcal{C}$REAMY PASTA & VEGGIE SALAD

Time: 95 minutes   Servings: 16

Ingredients:

2 tablespoons olive oil, divided

4 medium zucchinis, sliced into ½-inch thick rounds

4 small eggplants, sliced into ½-inch thick rounds

6 medium tomatoes, cut in eighths

4 fresh basil leaves, chopped

8 cups cooked shell pasta

½ cup fat-free Italian dressing

Salt, to taste

½ cup Parmesan cheese, grated

Directions:

Preheat the air fryer to 355 degrees F.

In a bowl, add zucchini and 1 tablespoon of oil and toss to coat well.

Place the zucchini slices in an Airfryer basket.

Cook for about 25 minutes.

Keep aside.

In a bowl, add eggplant and 1 tablespoon of oil and toss to coat well.

Place the eggplant slices in an Airfryer basket.

Cook for about 40 minutes.

Keep aside.

Now, set the Airfryer to 320 degrees F.

Grease the Airfryer basket with cooking spray.

Place tomato into the prepared basket.

Cook for about 30 minutes.

In a large bowl, mix together cooked vegetables and remaining all ingredients.

Cover and refrigerate for at least two hours before serving

TANGY PASTA & VEGGIE SALAD

Time: 30 minutes   Servings: 8

Ingredients:

2 orange bell pepper, seeded and chopped
2 green bell pepper, seeded and chopped
2 red bell pepper, seeded and chopped
1 red onion, minced
1 tablespoon fresh basil, chopped
Salt and freshly ground black pepper, to taste

¼ cup plus 1 tablespoon olive oil, divided
1 pound cooked penne pasta
1 cup cherry tomatoes, halved
½ cup olives
3 tablespoons balsamic vinegar

Directions:

Preheat the air fryer to 380 degrees F.

In a large bowl, add the peppers, red, basil, salt, black pepper and 1 tablespoon of oil and toss to coat well.

Grease the Airfryer basket with cooking spray.

Place the veggies into the prepared basket.

Cook for about 12-15 minutes.

In a large bowl, add cooked pasta, vegetables, tomatoes and olives, vinegar and remaining oil and toss to coat.

MAC AND CHEESE

Time: 35 minutes   Servings: 4

Ingredients:

2 cup shredded cheddar cheese, divided
1 teaspoon cornstarch
2 cup heavy whipping cream
2 cup dry macaroni

Directions:

In a bowl, mix together 1½ cups of cheese and cornstarch. Keep aside.

In another bowl, add remaining cheese, whipping cream and macaroni and mix well.

Transfer the macaroni mixture in baking pan.

With a piece of foil, cover the pan.

Preheat the Airfryer to 310 degrees F.

Place baking pan in an Airfryer basket.

Cook for about 15 minutes

Remove the foil and top with cornstarch mixture.

Place the pan, uncovered in Airfryer basket.

Cook for about10 minutes.

FOUR CHEESE MAC AND CHEESE

Time: 55 minutes   Servings: 6

Ingredients:

12-ounce dried macaroni pasta
2 tablespoons butter
2 tablespoons all-purpose flour
2½ cups half-and-half
1 cup Cheddar cheese, shredded
1 cup Fontina cheese, shredded
½ cup Gouda cheese, shredded

1/3 cup blue cheese, crumbled
Pinch of ground nutmeg
Salt and freshly ground black pepper, to taste
1 teaspoon butter, melted
¼ cup panko breadcrumbs

Directions:

In a large pan of lightly salted boiling water, cook the pasta for about 8 minutes.

Drain and keep aside.

Meanwhile in a large pan, melt the butter on medium heat.

Slowly, add the flour, stirring continuously.

Cook, stirring continuously for about 1-2 minutes.

Add the half-and-half and beat till smooth.

Bring the mixture to a boil.

Reduce the heat and simmer for about 5 minutes.

Meanwhile in a bowl, mix together Cheddar, Fontina and Gouda cheeses.

Reserve ½ cup of cheese mixture.

Remove from the heat and add the remaining cheese mixture and stir till melted.

Add the blue cheese, pinch of nutmeg, salt and pepper and stir till smooth.

Add the breadcrumbs and the melted butter in the bowl of reserved ½ cup cheese mixture and toss to combine.

Preheat the Airfryer to 360 degrees F.

In a 1½-quart ceramic baking dish, mix together the drained hot pasta and cheese sauce.

Sprinkle the ½ cup of c breadcrumbs mixture on top.

With a piece of foil, cover the baking dish.

Arrange the baking dish into Airfryer basket.

Cook for about 20 minutes.

Remove the foil and cook for about 5 minutes more.

FIVE CHEESE MAC AND CHEESE

Time: 45 minutes   Servings: 8

Ingredients:

½ pound dried macaroni pasta
½ cup whole milk
½ cup heavy cream
1/3 cup Fontina cheese, grated
1/3 cup Gruyere cheese, grated
1/3 cup sharp cheddar cheese, grated
1/3 cup mozzarella cheese, grated

½ teaspoon Emeril's Original Essence
Salt and freshly ground black pepper, to taste
1/8 teaspoon ground nutmeg
¼ cup bread crumbs
¼ cup Parmesan cheese, grated finely
1 tablespoon unsalted butter, melted

Directions:

In a large pan of lightly salted boiling water, cook the pasta for about 8 minutes.

Drain and transfer into a bowl.

Add the milk, heavy cream, Fontina, Gruyere, cheddar, mozzarella, Essence, salt, black pepper and nutmeg and stir till well combined.

In another small bowl, add the bread crumbs, Parmesan cheese and butter and stir to combine.

Transfer the macaroni mixture into a deep casserole dish.

Sprinkle with the breadcrumb mixture evenly.

Preheat the air fryer to 350 degrees F.

Arrange the casserole dish into Airfryer basket.

Cook for about 30 minutes.

SEAFOOD WITH PASTA

Time: 25 minutes   Servings: 4

Ingredients:

14-ounce shell pasta
4 tablespoons pesto, divided
4 (4-ounce) salmon steaks
2 tablespoons olive oil

½ pound cherry tomatoes, halved
8 large prawns, peeled and deveined
2 tablespoons fresh lemon juice
2 tablespoons fresh thyme, chopped

Directions:

In a large pan of lightly salted boiling water, add pasta and cook for about 8-10 minutes or till desired doneness.

Drain well and keep aside.

Meanwhile in the bottom of a baking dish, spread 1 tablespoon of the pesto

Place salmon steaks and tomatoes over pesto in a single layer.

Drizzle with oil evenly.

Top with prawns evenly.

Drizzle with lemon juice and sprinkle with thyme.

Preheat the Airfryer to 390 degrees F.

Cook for about 8 minutes.

Serve the seafood mixture with pasta.

Spaghetti with Mushrooms

Time: 40 minutes   Servings: 2

Ingredients:

1 teaspoon butter, melted
2 garlic cloves, chopped
9-ounce white button mushrooms
12-ounce carbonara mushroom sauce

2/3 cup water
Salt and freshly ground black pepper, to taste
10-ounce spaghetti

Directions:

Preheat the Airfryer at 285 degrees F.

Place a 6-inch pan in Airfryer for about 5 minutes while heating.

Coat the pan with butter evenly and place in the Airfryer.

Add garlic and cook for about 5 minutes.

Add mushrooms and cook for about 3 minutes.

Add carbonara sauce, water, salt and black pepper and mix well.

Cook for about 18 minutes, stirring occasionally.

Meanwhile in a large pan of lightly salted boiling water, add spaghetti and cook for about 8-10 minutes or till desired doneness.

Drain well.

Divide the spaghetti in serving plates.

Top with mushroom sauce and stir to combine before serving.

Mushroom Meatloaf

Time: 40 minutes   Servings: 4

Ingredients:

14-ounce lean ground beef
1 chorizo sausage, chopped finely
1 small onion, chopped
1 garlic clove, minced
2 tablespoons fresh cilantro, chopped
3 tablespoons breadcrumbs

1 egg
Salt and freshly ground black pepper, to taste
2 tablespoons fresh mushrooms, sliced thinly
2 tablespoons olive oil

Directions:

Preheat the Airfryer to 390 degrees F.

In a large bowl, add all ingredients except mushrooms and mix till well combined.

In a baking pan, place the beef mixture.

With the back of spatula, smooth the surface.

Top with mushroom slices and gently, press into the meatloaf.

Drizzle with oil evenly.

Arrange the pan in an Airfryer basket.

Cook for about 25 minutes.

Cut the meatloaf in desires size wedges and serve.

CHICKEN POT PIE

Time: 35 minutes   Servings: 4

Ingredients:

6 chicken tender pieces, chopped
1½ cups condensed cream of mushroom soup
2 potatoes, peeled and chopped
2/3 cup heavy cream

1 bay leaf
¼ teaspoon dried thyme, crushed
1 egg yolk
1 tablespoon milk
1 pre-made biscuit dough

Directions:

In a pan, add the chicken, condensed soup, potatoes, heavy cream, bay leaf, and thyme and bring to a boil.

Reduce the heat to medium-low and simmer for about 10-15 minutes.

In a small bowl, add egg yolk and milk and beat well.

In 4 small Airfryer safe small bowls, arrange the biscuit dough into 4 moulds.

Coat the dough moulds with egg wash.

Preheat the Airfryer to 360 degrees F.

Cook for about 5-7 minutes.

Remove the biscuit dough from Airfryer.

Divide the chicken mixture between the 4 biscuits dough evenly.

Cook for about 3-4 minutes.

BEEF POT PIE

Time: 100 minutes   Servings: 2

Ingredients:

1 tablespoon olive oil
1 pound beef stewing steak, cubed
1 large onion, chopped
1 tablespoon tomato puree
1 can ale
Warm water, as required
2 beef bouillon cubes

Salt and freshly ground black pepper, to taste
1 tablespoon plain flour plus more for dusting
1 prepared short crust pastry

Directions:

In a pan, heat oil on medium heat.

Add steak and cook for about 4-5 minutes.

Add onion and cook for about 4-5 minutes.

Add tomato puree and cook for about 2-3 minutes.

In a jug, add the ale and enough water to double the mixture.

Add the ale mixture, cubes, salt and black pepper in the pan with beef and bring to a boil on high heat.

Reduce the heat to low and simmer for about 1 hour.

In a bowl, mix together flour and 3 tablespoons of warm water.

Slowly, add the flour mixture in beef mixture, stirring continuously.

Remove from heat and keep aside.

Roll out the short crust pastry.

Line 2 ramekins with pastry and dust with flour.

Divide the beef mixture in the ramekins evenly.

Place extra pastry on top.

Preheat the Airfryer to 390 degrees F.

Cook for about 10 minutes.

Now, set the Airfryer to 335 degrees F.

Cook for about 6 minutes more.

Sausage Casserole

Time: 45 minutes

Servings: 4

Ingredients:

1 tablespoon olive oil
6-ounce flour
2 eggs
1 red onion, sliced thinly
1 garlic clove, minced

Salt and freshly ground black pepper, to taste
¾ cup milk
2/3 cup cold water
8 small sausages
8 fresh rosemary sprigs

Directions:

Grease a baking dish with olive oil.

In a bowl, sift the flour.

Add eggs and mix till well combined.

Stir in onion, garlic, rosemary, salt and black pepper.

Slowly, add milk and water and mix till well combined.

In each sausage, pierce 1 rosemary sprig.

Preheat the Airfryer to 320 degrees F.

Arrange the sausages in the prepared baking dish.

Top with the flour mixture evenly.

Cook for about 30 minutes.

POTATO GRATIN

Time: 35 minutes

Servings: 4

Ingredients:
2 large potatoes, sliced thinly
5 tablespoon plus 1 teaspoon coconut cream

2 eggs
1 tablespoon plain flour
½ cup cheddar cheese, grated

Directions:
Preheat the Airfryer to 355 degrees F. Arrange the potato slices in Airfryer.
Cook for about 10 minutes.
Meanwhile in a bowl, add coconut cream, eggs and flour and mix till a thick sauce forms.
Remove the potatoes from Airfryer. Now, place the potato slices in 4 ramekins evenly.
Top with the egg mixture evenly and sprinkle with cheese. Now, set the Airfryer to 390 degrees F.
Cook for about 10 minutes more.

TWO CHEESE POTATO GRATIN

Time: 30 minutes

Servings: 4

Ingredients:
¼ cup cream
¼ cup whole milk
1 teaspoon onion powder
1 teaspoon garlic powder
Freshly ground black pepper, to taste

3 medium russet potatoes, peeled and slice thinly
¼ cup Asiago cheese, shredded
¼ cup Gruyere cheese, shredded

Directions:
In a bowl, mix together cream, milk, onion powder, garlic powder and black pepper.
Dip potato slices in cream mixture evenly and arrange in a 6-inch baking dish.
Sprinkle with both cheeses evenly.
Preheat the Airfryer to 390 degrees F.
Arrange the baking dish in Airfryer.
Cook for about 15 minutes.

VEGGIE STUFFED BEEF ROLLS

Time: 30 minutes

Servings: 4

Ingredients:
2 pound beef flank steak, pounded to 1/8-inch thickness
3 tablespoons prepared pesto
6 Provolone cheese slices

3-ounce roasted red bell peppers
¾ cup fresh baby spinach
Salt and freshly ground black pepper, to taste

Directions:

Arrange the steak onto a smooth surface.

Spread the pesto over steak evenly.

Place the cheese slices over steak, followed by red peppers and spinach.

Roll up the steak around filling tightly.

Secure with the toothpicks.

Preheat the Airfryer to 400 degrees F.

Arrange the roll in Airfryer basket.

Cook for about 14 minutes, flipping once in the middle way.

Tomato Stuffed Pork Roll

Time: 35 minutes   Servings: 4

Ingredients:

1 scallion, chopped

¼ cup sun-dried tomatoes, chopped finely

2 tablespoons fresh parsley, chopped

Salt and freshly ground black pepper, to taste

4 (6-ounce) pork cutlets, pounded slightly

2 teaspoons paprika

½ tablespoon olive oil

Directions:

In a bowl, mix together, scallion, tomatoes, parsley, salt and black pepper.

Coat each cutlet with tomato mixture.

Roll each cutlet and secure with cocktail sticks.

Rub the outer part of rolls with paprika, salt and black pepper.

Coat the rolls with oil evenly.

Preheat the Airfryer to 390 degrees F.

Place the rolls in an Airfryer basket.

Cook for about 15 minutes.

Ham Stuffed Veal Rolls

Time: 30 minutes   Servings: 2

Ingredients:

4 (6-ounce) veal cutlets

Salt and freshly ground black pepper, to taste

2 tablespoons fresh sage leaves

4 cured ham slices

1 tablespoon unsalted butter, melted

Directions:

Preheat the Airfryer to 390 degrees F.

Season the veal cutlets with salt

Tightly, roll the veal cutlets and wrap each one with 1 ham slice.

Coat each roll with 1 tablespoon of the butter.

Place the sage leaves over each cutlet evenly.
Place the rolls in an Airfryer basket.
Cook for about 10 minutes.
Now, set the Airfryer to 300 degrees F.
Cook for about 5 minutes more.

*T*URKEY BREAST ROLLS

Time: 60 minutes   Servings: 4

Ingredients:
1 pound turkey breast fillet
1 garlic clove, crushed
1½ teaspoons ground cumin
1 teaspoon ground cinnamon
½ teaspoon red chili powder

Salt, to taste
2 tablespoons olive oil
3 tablespoons fresh parsley, chopped finely
1 small red onion, chopped finely

Directions:
Place the turkey fillet on a cutting board.
Carefully, cut horizontally along the length about 1/3 of the way from the top, stopping about ¼-inch from the edge.
Open this part to have a long piece of fillet.
In a bowl, mix together garlic, spices and oil.
Reserve about 1 tablespoon of oil.
In the remaining oil mixture, mix together parsley and onion.
Preheat the Airfryer to 355 degrees F.
Coat the open side of fillet with onion mixture.
Tightly, roll the fillet from the short side.
With kitchen string, tire the roll at 1-1½-inch intervals.
Coat the outer side of roll with remaining spice mixture.
Place the roll in Airfryer and cook for about 40 minutes.

*S*AUSAGE ROLLS

Time: 40 minutes   Servings: 4

Ingredients:
3-ounce butter
1½ cups plain flour
1 teaspoon parsley
Salt and freshly ground black pepper, to taste
1 tablespoon vegetable oil
Water, as required
1 teaspoon mustard seeds

9-ounce sausage meat
1 egg, beaten

Directions:

For pastry in a food processor, add butter, flour, parsley, salt and black pepper and pulse till the mixture resembles breadcrumbs.

Slowly, add the vegetable oil and the water and pulse till a dough is formed.

Place the dough onto floured surface and knead till smooth.

Roll the dough into a thin pastry.

Spread the mustard seeds over the pastry.

Now, place the sausage meat in a line through the center of the pastry and brush the edges with the egg.

Roll the sausage rolls and cut them into small portions.

Brush the top and sides with the egg.

Preheat the Airfryer to 325 degrees F.

Place the rolls in the Airfryer.

Cook the sausage rolls for about 20 minutes.

Now, set the Airfryer to 400 degrees F.

Cook for about 5 minutes more.

HAM ROLLS

Time: 30 minutes   Servings: 2

Ingredients:

12-ounce refrigerated pizza crust
1/3 pound cooked ham, sliced
¾ cup Mozzarella cheese, shredded
3 cups Colby cheese, shredded

1 egg yolk
1 tablespoon nonfat milk
3-ounce roasted red bell peppers

Directions:

Roll pizza dough into ¼ inch thickness.

Place ham, cheeses and roasted peppers over one side of dough

Fold over to seal.

In a small bowl, mix together milk and egg.

Brush the dough with egg mixture evenly.

Preheat the Airfryer to 360 degrees F.

Place the roll into an Airfryer basket.

Cook for about 15 minutes, flipping after every 5 minutes

HAM PINWHEELS

Time: 25 minutes   Servings: 4

Ingredients

1 puff pastry sheet
4 teaspoons Dijon mustard
10 ham slices

1 cup Gruyere cheese, shredded plus more for sprinkling

Directions:

Place the puff pastry sheet onto a floured surface.

Spread the mustard over the puff pastry evenly.

Top with ham and cheese.

Roll the puff pastry by starting the short edge.

Wrap the rolled pastry in plastic wrap and freeze for about 30 minutes.

Preheat the Airfryer at 375 degrees F.

Line an Airfryer basket with parchment paper.

Remove the pastry from freezer and slice into ½-inch rounds.

Arrange the pinwheels in prepared basket.

Cook for about 8 minutes.

Remove the pinwheels from Airfryer and sprinkle with a little more cheese.

Cook for about 2-3 minutes more.

Snacks Recipes

KALE CHIPS

Time: 15 minutes   Servings: 4

Ingredients:
1 head fresh kale, stems and ribs removed and cut into 1½ inch pieces
1 tablespoon olive oil
1 teaspoon soy sauce

Directions:
Preheat the Airfryer to 390 degrees F.
In a large bowl, add all ingredients and toss to coat well.
Place the kale in the fryer basket.
Cook for about 2-3 minutes, tossing once in the middle way.

POTATO CHIPS

Time: 45 minutes   Servings: 4

Ingredients:
4 small russet potatoes, sliced thinly
1 tablespoon olive-oil

2 tablespoons fresh rosemary, chopped finely
¼ teaspoon salt

Directions:
In a large bowl, of water, oak the potatoes for about 30 minutes, changing water halfway through.
Drain well and pat dry with paper towels.
Preheat the Air-Fryer to 350 degrees.
In a bowl, add potato slices, olive oil, rosemary and salt and toss to coat.
Place the potato chips in Airfryer basket.
Cook for about 30 minutes.

APPLE CHIPS

Time: 25 minutes   Servings: 2

Ingredients:
1 apple, peeled, cored and thinly sliced
1 tablespoon sugar
½ teaspoon ground cinnamon
Pinch of ground ginger

Pinch of salt

Directions:

Preheat the Airfryer to 390 degrees F.

In a bowl, add all ingredients and toss to coat well.

Place the apple slices in an Airfryer basket in batches.

Cook for about 7-8 minutes, flipping once in the middle way.

Banana Chips

Time: 20 minutes   Servings: 8

Ingredients:

2 raw bananas, peeled and sliced   Salt and freshly ground pepper, to taste
2 tablespoons olive oil

Directions:

Preheat the air fryer to 355 degrees F.

Drizzle the banana slices with oil evenly.

Place the banana slice in Airfryer and cook for about 10 minutes.

Sprinkle with salt and black pepper.

Preserve in an airtight jar.

Tortilla Chips

Time: 15 minutes   Servings: 6

Ingredients:

8 corn tortillas, cut into triangles   Salt, to taste
1 tablespoon olive oil

Directions:

Preheat the air fryer to 390 degrees F.

Coat the tortilla chips with oil.

Arrange the chips in Airfryer basket in batches.

Cook for about 3 minutes.

Roosted Cashews

Time: 20 minutes   Servings: 8

Ingredients:

2 cups raw cashew nuts   Salt and freshly ground black pepper, to
1 teaspoon butter, melted   taste

Directions:

Preheat the Airfryer to 355 degrees F.

In a bowl, add all ingredients and toss to coat well.

In an Airfryer basket, place the cashews.
Cook for about 4 minutes, shaking once uin the middle way.

ROOSTED NUTS

Time: 20 minutes

Servings: 10

Ingredients:
1¼ cups raw peanuts
1¼ cups raw almonds

1 tablespoon olive oil
Salt, to taste

Directions:
Preheat the Airfryer at 320 degrees F.
In an Airfryer basket, place the nuts.
Cook for about 9 minutes, tossing twice.
Remove the nuts from Airfryer basket and transfer into a bowl.
Add oil and salt sand toss to coat well.
Return the nuts mixture into Airfryer basket.
Cook for about 5 minutes.

ROASTED CHICKPEAS

Time: 20 minutes

Servings: 4

Ingredients:
1 (15-ounce) can chickpeas, rinsed and drained
1 tablespoon olive oil
½ teaspoon ground cumin

½ teaspoon cayenne pepper
½ teaspoon smoked paprika
Salt, taste

Directions:
Preheat the Airfryer to 390 degrees F.
In a bowl, add all ingredients and toss to coat well.
Place the chickpeas in a fryer basket in batches.
Working in 2 batches Working in 2 batchesCook for about 8-10 minutes.

BUTTERED CORN

Time: 50 minutes

Servings: 2

Ingredients:
2 corn on the cob
Salt and freshly ground pepper, to taste
2 tablespoons butter, softened and divided

Directions:

Preheat the Airfryer to 320 degrees F.

Sprinkle the cobs with and black pepper evenly.

Rub with 1 tablespoon butter.

Wrap the cobs in foil paper and place in Airfryer basket.

Cook for about 20 minutes.

Top with remaining butter and serve.

$\mathcal{P}$OLENTA STICKS

Time: 15 minutes   Servings: 4

Ingredients:

1 tablespoon oil   Salt, to taste
2½ cups cooked polenta   ¼ cup Parmesan cheese

Directions:

Preheat the air fryer at 350 degrees F.

Grease the baking dish with oil.

Place the polenta in a baking dish.

Cover and refrigerate for about 1 hour or till set.

Remove from the refrigerator and cut into desired sized slices.

Place the polenta sticks into the Airfryer.

Sprinkle with salt.

Cook for about 5-6 minutes.

Top with cheese and serve.

$\mathcal{E}$GGPLANT SLICES

Time: 30 minutes   Servings: 4

Ingredients:

1 medium eggplant, peeled and cut into   ¼ cup olive oil
½-inch round slices   1 cup Italian-style breadcrumbs
Salt, to taste   2 eggs, beaten
½ cup all-purpose flour

Directions:

Peel the eggplant and cut into round slices.

In a colander, place the eggplant slices and sprinkle with salt.

Keep aside for about 45 minutes.

Drain excess water with paper towels.

Preheat the Airfryer to 390 degrees F.

In a shallow dish, place the flour.

In a second shallow dish, beat the eggs.

In a third shallow dish, mix together oil and breadcrumbs.

Coat the eggplant slices into flour evenly.

Dip the eggplant slices into egg and then coat with breadcrumb mixture evenly.

Place the eggplant slices in an Airfryer basket in batches.

Cook for about 8 minutes.

CARROT STICKS

Time: 25 minutes

Servings: 2

Ingredients:

1 large carrot, peeled and cut into sticks

1 tablespoon fresh rosemary, chopped finely

1 tablespoon olive oil

2 teaspoons sugar

¼ teaspoon cayenne pepper

Salt and freshly ground black pepper, to taste

Directions:

Preheat the Airfryer to 390 degrees F.

In a bowl, add all ingredients and toss to coat well.

Place the carrot sticks in an Airfryer basket.

Cook for about 12 minutes.

CRAB STICKS

Time: 25 minutes

Servings: 4

Ingredients:

1 packet crab sticks

2 teaspoon sesame oil

Cajun seasoning, to taste

Directions:

Preheat the Airfryer at 320 degrees F.

Break each crab stick lengthways and then shred into small pieces.

In a bowl, add crab stick pieces and drizzle with oil evenly.

Place the crab stick pieces in an Airfryer basket.

Cook for about 12 minutes.

Sprinkle with seasoning and serve.

ZUCCHINI FRIES

Time: 30 minutes

Servings: 4

Ingredients:

1 pound zucchinis, sliced into 2 ½ inch sticks

Salt, to taste

2 tablespoons olive oil

¾ cup panko bread crumbs

Directions:

In a colander, place the zucchini and sprinkle with salt.
Keep aside for about 10 minutes.
Preheat the Airfryer to 390 degrees F.
With the paper towels, gently dry the zucchini fries.
In a shallow dish, place the bread crumb.
Coat the zucchini fries in breadcrumbs evenly.
Place the zucchini in a fryer basket in batches.
Cook for about 10 minutes.

Potato Fries

Time: 40 minutes   Servings: 4

Ingredients:

1¾ pound potatoes, peeled and cut into   1 teaspoon onion powder
thin strips   1 teaspoon garlic powder
¼ cup olive oil   2 teaspoons paprika

Directions:

In a large bowl of cold water, place the potato strips for about 1 hour.
Drain well and pat dry with paper towels.
In a large bowl and potato strips and remaining ingredients and toss to coat well.
Preheat the air fryer to 375 degrees F. Cook for about 30 minutes.

Sweet Potato Fries

Time: 25 minutes   Servings: 2

Ingredients:

2 large sweet potatoes, peeled and cut into thin strips
1 tablespoon olive oil.

Directions:

Preheat the air fryer to 355 degrees F.
Coat the sweet potato fries with oil evenly.
Place the sweet potato fries in Airfryer.
Cook for about 15 minutes.

Avocado Fries

Time: 25 minutes   Servings: 3

Ingredients:

½ cup panko breadcrumbs   Liquid from bean can, as required
Salt, to taste   1 Haas avocado, peeled, pitted and sliced

Directions:

In a shallow bowl, mix together panko and salt.

In another shallow dish, place the can liquid.

Dip the avocado slices in can liquid and then cat with breadcrumb mixture evenly.

Preheat the air fryer to 390 degrees F.

Place the fries in Airfryer.

Cook for about 10 minutes, shaking after every 5 minutes.

BUTTERNUT SQUASH FRIES

Time: 55 minutes   Servings: 4

Ingredients:

2 pound butternut squash, peeled and cut into ½ inch strips

1 teaspoon chili powder

½ teaspoon ground cinnamon

¼ teaspoon garlic salt

Directions:

Preheat the Airfryer to 390 degrees F.

Grease the Airfryer with cooking spray.

In a large bowl, add all ingredients and toss to coat well.

Place the butternut squash fries in Airfryer.

Cook for about 35-40 minutes until golden browned.

CAULIFLOWER POPPERS

Time: 25 minutes   Servings: 4

Ingredients:

¼ cup golden raisins

1 cup boiling water

½ cup olive oil, divided

¼ cup toasted pine nuts

1 head of cauliflower, cut into small florets

1 tablespoon curry powder

¼ teaspoon salt

Directions:

Preheat the Airfryer to 390 degrees F.

In a bowl, add raisins and boiling water and keep aside.

In a bowl, add pine nuts with 1 teaspoon olive oil.

Place the pine nuts in an Airfryer basket.

Cook for about 1-2 minutes.

Remove from the Airfryer and keep aside.

In a bowl, mix together cauliflower, curry powder, salt and remaining oil.

Transfer to the fryer basket. Cook for about 8-10 minutes

Darin raisins.

In a serving bowl, mix together cauliflower, raisins and pine nuts and serve.

*B*ROCCOLI POPPERS

Time: 40 minutes   Servings: 2

Ingredients:

2 tablespoons plain yogurt
½ teaspoon red chili powder
¼ teaspoon ground cumin
¼ teaspoon ground turmeric

Salt, to taste
1 pound broccoli, cut into small florets
2 tablespoons chickpea flour

Directions:

In a bowl, mix together yogurt and spices. Add broccoli and coat with the marinade generously.
Refrigerate for about 20 minutes. Preheat the Airfryer to 400 degrees F.
Sprinkle the broccoli florets with chickpea floor evenly.
Place the broccoli in the Airfryer basket. Cook for about 10 minutes, tossing once in the middle way.
Serve hot.

*O*NION RINGS

Time: 20 minutes   Servings: 4

Ingredients:

1 large onion, cut into ¼ inch slices
1 ¼ cups all-purpose flour
1 teaspoon baking powder
Salt, to taste

1 cup milk
1 egg
¾ cup dry bread crumbs

Directions:

Preheat the Airfryer to 360 degrees F.
Separate the onion slices into rings.
In a shallow dish, mix together flour, baking powder and salt.
In a second shallow dish, add milk and egg and beat well.
In a third shallow dish, place the breadcrumbs.
Coat the onion rings into flour mixture.
Dip the onion rings into egg mixture and then coat with breadcrumbs evenly.
Place the onion rings in air fryer and cook for about 7-10 minutes.

*R*ISOTTO BITES

Time: 35 minutes   Servings: 4

Ingredients:

3 cups cooked risotto
1/3 cup Parmesan cheese, grated
1 egg, beaten

3-ounce mozzarella cheese, cubed
¾ cup bread crumbs

Directions:

In a bowl, add risotto, Parmesan and egg and mix till well combined.

Make 20 equal-sized balls from the mixture.

Insert a mozzarella cube in the center of each ball.

With your fingers smooth the risotto mixture to cover the ball.

In a shallow dish, place the bread crumbs.

Coat the balls in bread crumbs evenly.

Preheat the Airfryer to 390 degrees F.

Place the balls in an Airfryer basket in batches

Cook for about 10 minutes or till golden browned.

Cheesy Rice Bites

Time: 25 minutes   Servings: 4

Ingredients:

6 tablespoons milk

½ teaspoon vegetable oil

¾ cup rice flour

1 ounce Parmesan cheese

Directions:

Preheat the Airfryer to300 degrees F.

In a bowl, add milk, flour, oil and cheese and mix till a smooth dough forms.

Make small balls from the dough. Place the balls in an Airfryer basket.

Cook for about 12 minutes or till done.

Mixed Veggie Bites

Time: 30 minutes   Servings: 10

Ingredients:

1½ pound fresh spinach, blanched, drained and chopped

½ of onion, chopped

1 carrot, peeled and chopped

1 garlic clove, minced

2 American cheese slices, cut into tiny pieces

2 bread slices, toasted and processed into breadcrumbs

1 tablespoon corn flour

1 teaspoon red chili flakes

Salt, to taste

Directions:

Preheat the Airfryer at 355 degrees F.

In a bowl, add all ingredients except breadcrumbs and mix till well combined.

Add breadcrumbs and gently mix to combine. Make 20 equal-sized balls from the mixture.

Preheat the air fryer at 200 degrees C

Place the balls in an Airfryer basket.

Cook for about 10 minutes.

BROCCOLI BITES

Time: 30 minutes

Servings: 10

Ingredients:

2 cups broccoli florets
2 eggs, beaten
1¼ cups cheddar cheese, grated
¼ cup Parmesan cheese, grated

1¼ cups panko breadcrumbs
Salt and freshly ground black pepper, to taste

Directions:

In a food processor, add broccoli and pulse till crumbed finely.
In a large bowl, broccoli and remaining ingredients and mix till well combined.
Make small equal-sized balls from mixture.
Arrange the balls in a baking sheet and refrigerate for at least 30 minutes.
Preheat the air fryer to 350 degrees F.
Place the balls in a fryer basket
Cook for about 12 minutes.

COD NUGGETS

Time: 25 minutes

Servings: 4

Ingredients:

1 cup all-purpose flour
2 eggs
¾ cup breadcrumbs

Pinch of salt
2 tablespoons olive oil
1 pound cod, cut into 1x2½-inch strips

Directions:

Preheat the Airfryer to 390 degrees F.
In a shallow dish, place the flour.
In a second shallow dish, beat the eggs.
In a third shallow dish, mix together breadcrumbs, salt and oil.
Coat the fish strips in flour evenly.
Dip in eggs and then roll into breadcrumbs mixture evenly.
Arrange the croquettes in an Airfryer basket.
Cook for about 8-10 minutes.

CHICKEN & VEGGIE NUGGETS

Time: 25 minutes

Servings: 4

Ingredients:

½ of zucchini, chopped roughly
½ of carrot, chopped roughly

14-ounce chicken breast, cut into chunks
½ tablespoon mustard powder

1 tablespoon garlic powder
1 tablespoon onion powder
Salt and freshly ground black pepper, to taste

1 cup all-purpose flour
2 tablespoons milk
1 egg
1 cup panko breadcrumbs

Directions:

In a food processor, add zucchini and carrot and pulse till chopped finely.

Add chicken, mustard powder, garlic powder, onion powder, salt and black pepper and pulse till combined.

Preheat the Airfryer to 390 degrees F. In a shallow dish, place the flour.

In a second shallow dish, beat the milk and egg.

In a third shallow dish, place the breadcrumbs.

Coat the nuggets in flour evenly.

Dip in egg mixture and then roll into breadcrumbs evenly.

Arrange the nuggets in an Airfryer basket.

Cook for about 10 minutes.

BACON CROQUETTES

Time: 25 minutes   Servings: 6

Ingredients:

1 pound thin bacon slices
1 pound sharp cheddar cheese block, cut into 1-inch rectangular pieces
1cup all-purpose flour

3 eggs
1 cup breadcrumbs
Salt, to taste
¼ cup olive oil

Directions:

Wrap 2 bacon slices around 1 piece of cheddar cheese, covering completely.

Repeat with the remaining bacon and cheese pieces.

Arrange the croquettes in a baking dish and freeze for about 5 mutes.

Preheat the Airfryer to 390 degrees F.

In a shallow dish, place the flour.

In a second shallow dish, beat the eggs.

In a third shallow dish, mix together breadcrumbs, salt and oil.

Coat the croquettes in flour evenly.

Dip in eggs and then roll into breadcrumbs mixture evenly.

Arrange the croquettes in an Airfryer basket.

Cook for about 7-8 minutes.

SALMON CROQUETTES

Time: 30 minutes   Servings: 16

Ingredients:

I large can red salmon, drained

2 eggs, lightly beaten

2 tablespoons fresh parsley, chopped
Salt and freshly ground black pepper, to taste

1/3 cup vegetable oil
1 cup bread crumbs

Directions:

Preheat the Airfryer to 390 degrees F. In a bowl, add salmon and mash completely.
Add egg, parsley, salt and black pepper and mix till well combined.
Make 16 equal-sized croquettes from the mixture. In a shallow dish, mix together oil and breadcrumbs.
Coat croquettes in breadcrumb mixture. Place the croquettes in an Airfryer basket in batches.
Cook for about 7 minutes.

POTATO CROQUETTES

Time: 25 minutes

Servings: 14

Ingredients:

2 medium Russet potatoes, peeled and cubed
2 tablespoons all-purpose flour
½ cup Parmesan cheese, grated
1 egg yolk
2 tablespoons chives, minced

Pinch of ground nutmeg
Salt and freshly ground black pepper, to taste
2 eggs
½ cup breadcrumbs
2 tablespoons vegetable oil

Directions:

In a pan of salted water, boil the potatoes for about 15 minutes.
Drain well and mash the potatoes completely.
Transfer the potatoes in a large bowl and keep aside to cool completely.
Add Parmesan, egg yolk, chives, nutmeg, salt and black pepper and mix till well combined.
Make equal sized small balls from the mixture. In a shallow dish, beat eggs.
In another shallow dish, mix together breadcrumbs and oil.
Dip each ball into egg and then roll into breadcrumbs mixture evenly.
Then roll the balls into cylinder shape.
Preheat the Airfryer to 390 degrees F.
Arrange the croquettes in an Airfryer basket.
Cook for about 7-8 minutes.

SPINACH STUFFED BREAD ROLLS

Time: 25 minutes

Servings: 18

Ingredients:

5 large potatoes, peeled
2 tablespoons vegetable oil, divided
2 small onions, chopped finely
2 green chilies, seeded and chopped

2 curry leaves
½ teaspoon ground turmeric
Salt, to taste
8 bread slices, trimmed

Directions:

In a large pan of salted boiling water, cook the potatoes for about 15-20 minutes.
Drain well and mash completely. In a skillet, heat 1 teaspoon of oil on medium heat.
Add onion and sauté for about 4-5 minutes.
Add green chilies, curry leaves and turmeric and sauté for about 1 minute.
Add mashed potatoes and salt and stir to combine.
Remove from heat and keep aside to cool completely.
Make 8 equal sized oval shaped patties from the mixture.
Wet the bread slices with water completely.
Press each bread slices between your hands to remove the excess water.
Place 1 bread slice in your palm and arrange 1 patty in the center.
Roll the bread slice in a spindle shape and seal the edges to secure the filling.
Cot the roll with some oil. Repeat with the remaining slices, filling and oil.
Preheat the Airfryer to 390 degrees F. Grease the Airfryer basket with cooking spray.
Place the rolls into the prepared Airfryer basket.
Cook for about 12-13 minutes.

Mozzarella Sticks

Time: 25 minutes   Servings: 4

Ingredients:

¼ cup white flour
2 eggs
3 tablespoon nonfat milk

1 cup plain bread crumbs
1 pound Mozzarella cheese block cut into
3x½-inch sticks

Directions:

In a shallow dish, place the flour. In a second shallow dish, add eggs and milk and beat well.
In a third shallow dish, place the breadcrumbs.
Coat the Mozzarella sticks in flour, then dip in egg mixture.
Now, coat with the bread crumbs.
Arrange the Mozzarella sticks onto a cookie sheet and freezer for about 1-2 hours.
Preheat the Airfryer to 400 degrees F.
Place the Mozzarella sticks in Airfryer basket in batches.
Cook for about 12 minutes.

Cheese Pastries

Time: 25 minutes   Servings: 6

Ingredients:

1 egg yolk
4-ounce feta cheese, crumbled
1 scallion, chopped finely
2 tablespoons fresh parsley, chopped finely

Salt and freshly ground black pepper, to
taste
2 frozen filo pastry sheets, thawed
2 tablespoons olive oil

Directions:

In a large bowl, add the egg yolk and beat well.

Add feta, scallion, parsley, salt and black pepper and mix well.

Cut each filo pastry sheet in three strips.

Place about 1 teaspoon of the feta mixture on the underside of a strip.

Fold the tip of the sheet over filling in a zigzag manner to form a triangle.

Repeat with the remaining strips and filling.

Preheat the Airfryer to 390 degrees F.

Coat each pastry with oil evenly.

Place the pastries in an Airfryer basket.

Cook for about 3 minutes.

Now, set the Airfryer to 360 degrees F.

Cook for about 2 minutes.

VEGGIE PASTRIES

Time: 30 minutes   Servings: 8

Ingredients:

2 large potatoes, peeled
1 tablespoon olive oil
½ cup carrot, peeled and chopped
½ cup onion, chopped
2 garlic cloves, minced
2 tablespoons fresh ginger, minced

½ cup green peas, shelled
1 tablespoon curry powder
Salt and freshly ground black pepper, to taste
3 puff pastry sheets

Directions:

In a pan of salted water, cook the potatoes for about 15-20 minutes.

Drain well and mash completely.

In a skillet, heat oil on medium heat.

Add carrot, onion, ginger and garlic and sauté for about 4-5 minutes.

Drain any fat from the skillet.

Stir in the mashed potatoes.

Add peas, curry powder, salt and black pepper and cook for about 1-2 minutes.

Cut each puff pastry sheet into 4 pieces and then cut each piece in a round shape.

Place about 2 tablespoons of veggie filling over each pastry round.

With your wet fingers, moisten the edges.

Fold each pastry round in half to seal the filling.

With a fork, press the edges firmly.

Preheat the Airfryer to 390 degrees F.

In an Airfryer basket, place the pastries in batches.

Cook for about 5 minutes.

CHOCOLATY SQUARES

Time: 35 minutes

Servings: 8

Ingredients:

3½-ounce cold butter
2½-ounce brown sugar
6-ounce self-rising flour

¼ cup honey
3½-ounce chocolate, chopped
1 tablespoon milk

Directions:

Preheat the Airfryer at 320 degrees F. In a large bowl, add the butter and beat till soft.
Add brown sugar and beat till smooth. Add flour and honey and mix till well combined.
Add the chocolate and milk and mix till well combined.
Place the mixture into a tin and arrange the tin in a baking sheet.
Arrange the baking sheet in an Airfryer basket. Cook for about 20 minutes.
Remove from Airfryer and keep aside to cool slightly.
Cut into desired squares and serve.

LEMON BISCUITS

Time: 20 minutes

Servings: 10

Ingredients:

8½ ounce self-rising flour
3½-ounce caster sugar
3½-ounce cold butter
1 small egg

1 teaspoon fresh lemon zest, grated finely
2 tablespoons fresh lemon juice
1 teaspoon vanilla extract

Directions:

In a large bowl, mix together flour and sugar.
With a pastry cutter, cut cold butter and mix till a coarse crumb forms.
Add egg, lemon zest and lemon juice and mix till a soft dough forms.
Place the dough onto a floured surface and roll the dough.
Cut the dough into medium-sized biscuits.
Arrange the biscuits in a baking sheet in a single layer.
Preheat the Airfryer at 355 degrees F.
Cook for about 5 minutes or till golden brown.

Buttermilk Biscuits

Time: 25 minutes

Servings: 4

Ingredients:

1¼ cups all-purpose flour
½ cup cake flour
¼ teaspoon baking soda
½ teaspoon baking powder
1 teaspoon granulated sugar

Salt, to taste
¼ cup cold unsalted butter, cut into cubes
¾ cup buttermilk
2 tablespoons butter, melted

Directions:

In a large bowl, sift together flours, baking soda, baking powder, sugar and salt.

With a pastry cutter, cut cold butter and mix till a coarse crumb forms.

Slowly, add buttermilk and mix till a smooth dough forms.

Place the dough onto a floured surface and with your hands, press it into ½ inch thickness.

With a 1¾-inch round cookie cutter, cut the biscuits.

Cut out the remaining biscuits with the dough.

Arrange the biscuits in a pie pan in a single layer and coat with the butter.

Preheat the Airfryer to 400 degrees F.

Cook for about 8 minutes or till golden brown.

Chocolaty Coconut Cookies

Time: 30 minutes

Servings: 8

Ingredients:

2¼-ounce caster sugar
3½-ounce butter
1 small egg
1 teaspoon vanilla extract

5-ounce self-rising flour
1¼-ounce white chocolate, chopped finely
3 tablespoons desiccated coconut

Directions:

Preheat the Airfryer to 355 degrees F.

In a large bowl, add sugar and butter and beat till fluffy and light.

Add egg and vanilla extract and beat till well combined.

Add flour and chocolate and mix till well combined.

In a shallow dish, place the coconut.

Make small balls from the mixture and roll into coconut evenly.

Place the balls onto baking sheet and gently, press each ball.

Place the baking sheet in an Airfryer basket.

Cook for about 8 minutes.

Now, set the Airfryer at 320 degrees F.

Cook for about 4 minutes.

BUTTERED COOKIES

Time: 25 minutes   Servings: 4

Ingredients:

4-ounce unsalted butter, softened   1 cup all-purpose flour
1¼-ounce icing sugar   ¼ teaspoon baking powder

Directions:

Preheat the Airfryer to 340 degrees F.
In a large bowl, add the butter and beat till soft.
Add icing sugar and beat till smooth.
Add flour and baking powder and beat till a sticky dough forms.
Place the dough into a piping bag fitted with a fluted nozzle.
Pipe the dough onto a baking sheet. In a single layer.
Arrange the baking sheet in an Airfryer basket.
Cook for about 8-10 minutes.

CHOCOLATY COOKIE BALLS

Time: 25 minutes   Servings: 6

Ingredients:

16½ ounce store-bought chocolate chip   ½ cup chocolate cookie crumbs
cookie dough, chilled   2 tablespoons sugar
¼ cup butter, melted

Directions:

Divide and roll the chilled cookie dough into 12 balls.
In a shallow dish, place the melted butter.
In another shallow dish, mix together the cookie crumbs and sugar.
Dip each cookie ball in the melted butter and then coat with the cookie crumbs evenly.
Place the coated cookie balls on a baking sheet and freeze for at least 2 hours.
Preheat the air fryer to 350 F.
Line the air fryer basket with a piece of foil.
Place the cookies balls onto prepared basket in batches.
Cook for about 10 minutes.

Dessert Recipes

STUFFED PEAR POUCH

Time: 25 minutes   Servings: 4

Ingredients:

2 small pears, peeled, cored and halved
2 cups vanilla custard
4 puff pastry sheets
1 egg, beaten lightly

2 tablespoons sugar
Pinch of ground cinnamon
2 tablespoons whipped cream

Directions:

Carefully, make small cuts in each pear half.
In the center of each pastry sheet, place a spoonful of vanilla custard and top with a pear half.
In a bowl, mix together sugar and cinnamon. Sprinkle the sugar mixture over pear halves evenly.
Pinch the corners to shape into a pouch. Preheat the Airfryer at 330 degrees F.
Place the pear pouches in an Airfryer basket.
Cook for about 15 minutes.
Top with whipped cream and serve with remaining custard.

STUFFED APPLES

Time: 25 minutes   Servings: 4

Ingredients:

For Stuffed Apples:
4 small firm apples, cored
½ cup golden raisins
½ cup blanched almonds
2 tablespoons sugar

For Vanilla Sauce:
½ cup whipped cream
2 tablespoons sugar
½ teaspoon vanilla extract

Directions:

Preheat the Airfryer to 355 degrees F.
Line a baking dish with a parchment paper.
In a food processor, add raisins, almond and sugar and pulse till chopped.
Carefully, stuff each apple with raisin mixture.
Arrange the apples in the prepared baking dish.
Place the baking dish in an Airfryer basket. Cook for about 10 minutes.
For vanilla sauce in a pan, add cream, sugar and vanilla extract on medium heat.
Cook, stirring continuously for about 2-3 minutes or till sugar is dissolved.
Remove from the heat and keep aside to cool.
Serve apple with vanilla sauce.

Nutty Banana Split

Time: 20 minutes   Servings: 8

Ingredients:

3 tablespoons coconut oil
1 cup panko bread crumbs
4 bananas, peeled and halved lengthwise
½ cup corn flour

2 eggs
3 tablespoons sugar
¼ teaspoon ground cinnamon
2 tablespoons walnuts, chopped

Directions:

In a skillet, heat oil on medium heat.
Add bread crumbs and cook for 3-4 minutes until golden browned and crumbled.
Transfer into a bowl and keep aside to cool.
In a shallow dish, place the flour.
In another shallow dish, beat the egg.
Coat banana slices with flour evenly.
Dip in egg and then coat with bread crumbs evenly.
In a small bowl, ix together the sugar and cinnamon
Preheat the air fryer at 280 degrees F.
Place the banana slices in an Airfryer basket.
Sprinkle with cinnamon sugar
Cook for about 10 minutes.
Serve with the sprinkling of walnuts.

Pineapple Sticks with Yogurt Dip

Time: 25 minutes   Servings: 4

Ingredients:

For Pineapple Sticks:
½ of pineapple
¼ cup desiccated coconut

For Yogurt Dip:
1 tablespoon fresh mint leaves, minced
1 cup vanilla yogurt

Directions:

Preheat the Airfryer to 390 degrees F.
Remove the outer skin of the pineapple and cut into long 1-2 inch thick sticks.
In a shallow dish place the coconut.
Coat the pineapple sticks in coconut evenly.
Place the pineapple sticks in an Airfryer basket.
Cook for about 10 minutes.
For dip in a bowl, mix together mint and yogurt.
Serve pineapple sticks with yogurt dip.

FRUIT MERINGUE

Time: 100 minutes   Servings: 4

Ingredients:
5 egg whites
2 teaspoons cornstarch, sieved
3½-ounce super-fine sugar, divided
1 papaya, peeled and chopped
1 mango, peeled, pitted and chopped

1 pineapple, peeled and chopped
4 passion fruit, chopped
1 teaspoon fresh lemon juice
1 cup whipped cream

Directions:
In a bowl, add egg whites and beat till fluffy.
Slowly, add the cornstarch and 2¾-ounce of sugar and beat till peaks form.
Cut 2 sheets from a parchment paper.
Divide the egg white mixture onto both sheets evenly.
Preheat the Airfryer to 210 degrees F.
Place 1 sheet in Airfryer grill pan.
Cook for about 1 hour.
Remove from Airfryer and keep aside to cool for about 5 minutes.
Repeat with the remaining sheet.
Carefully remove the egg white mixture from sheets.
Flip the side and keep aside to dry.
In a bowl, place about ¼ cup of each fruit and preserve them.
In a food processor, add remaining fruit and lemon juice and pulse till a puree forms.
In a bowl, add whipped cream and remaining sugar and beat till stiff.
Transfer the whipped cream in a piping bag with a star nozzle.
Place the reserve chopped fruit over meringue and top with fruit puree.
Decorate with whipped cream and serve.

VANILLA SOUFFLÉ

Time: 35 minutes   Servings: 3

Ingredients:
¼ cup butter, softened
¼ cup all-purpose flour
½ cup sugar
1 cup milk
3 teaspoons vanilla extract, divided

4 egg yolks
5 egg whites
1 teaspoon cream of tartar
1-ounce sugar

Directions:
In a bowl, add butter and flour and mix till a smooth paste forms.
In a pan, mix together ½ cup of sugar and milk on medium-low heat.
Cook, stirring continuously for about 2-3 minutes or till the sugar dissolves.

Bring to a boil and add the flour mixture, beating continuously.

Simmer for about 3-4 minutes or till mixture becomes thick.

Remove from heat and stir in 1 teaspoon of vanilla extract.

Keep aside for about 10 minutes to cool.

Grease 3 (6-ounce) ramekins and sprinkle with a pinch of sugar.

In a bowl, add egg yolks and vanilla extract and beat well.

Add the egg yolk mixture in milk mixture and mix till well combined.

In another bowl, add egg whites, cream of tartar, remaining sugar and vanilla extract and beat till stiff peaks form. Fold the egg whites mixture into milk mixture.

Divide the mixture into prepared ramekins and with the back of a spoon, smooth the top surface.

Preheat the Airfryer to 330 degrees F. Place 3 ramekins in Airfryer basket and cook for about 14-16 minutes.

Repeat with the remaining ramekins.

CHOCOLATE SOUFFLÉ

Time: 30 minutes
Servings: 2
¼ cup butter
3-ounce bittersweet chocolate, chopped

2 eggs, separated
3 tablespoons sugar
½ teaspoon pure vanilla extract
2 tablespoons all-purpose flour
Powdered sugar, for dusting

Directions:

In a microwave safe bowl, add butter and chocolate.

Microwave on high for about 2 minutes or till melted completely, stirring after every 30 seconds.

In another bowl, add the egg yolks and beat well. Add sugar and vanilla extract and beat well.

Add the chocolate mixture, and mix till well combined. Add the flour and mix till well combined.

In a small bowl, add egg whites and beat till soft peaks form. Preheat the Airfryer to 330 F.

Grease 2 (6-ounce) ramekins and dust with some powdered sugar.

Slowly, fold the whipped egg whites into chocolate mixture.

Transfer the mixture into prepared ramekins, leaving about ½- inch from the top.

Place the ramekins into the air fryer basket.

Cook for about 14 minutes.

Dust with powdered sugar and serve immediately.

CHERRY CLAFOUTIS

Time: 35 minutes

Servings: 4

Ingredients:

1½ cups fresh cherries, pitted
3 tablespoons vodka
¼ cup flour
2 tablespoons sugar
Pinch of salt

½ cup sour cream
1 egg
1 tablespoon butter
¼ cup powdered sugar

Directions:

In a bowl, mix together cherries and vodka.

In another bowl, mix together flour, sugar and salt.

Add sour cream and egg and mix till a smooth dough forms.

Preheat the Airfryer to 355 degrees F.

Grease a baking pan.

Transfer the flour mixture into prepared baking pan evenly.

Spread the cherry mixture over the dough evenly.

Place the butter on top in the form of dots.

Place the baking pan in an Airfryer basket.

Cook for about 25 minutes.

Sprinkle with powdered sugar and serve warm.

CHOCOLATE PUDDING

Time: 25 minutes   Servings: 4

Ingredients:

½ cup butter

2/3 cup dark chocolate, chopped

¼ cup caster sugar

2 medium eggs

2 teaspoons fresh orange rind, grated finely

¼ cup fresh orange juice

2 tablespoon self-rising flour

Directions:

Grease 4 ramekins.

In a microwave safe bowl, add butter and chocolate.

Microwave on high for about 2 minutes or till melted completely, stirring after every 30 seconds.

Remove bowl from microwave and stir the mixture till creamy.

In a small bowl, add sugar and eggs and beat till frothy.

Add orange rind, juice and egg mixture into the bowl of chocolate mixture and mix well.

Add flour and mix till well combined.

Preheat the Airfryer to 355 degrees F.

Transfer the mixture into prepared ramekins about ¾ full.

Cook for about 12 minutes.

CHOCOLATE BREAD PUDDING

Time: 25 minutes   Servings: 2

Ingredients:

1 cup milk

1 egg

1 tablespoon brown sugar

½ teaspoon ground cinnamon

¼ teaspoon vanilla extract

2 tablespoons raisins, soaked in hot water for about 15 minutes

2 bread slices, cut into small cubes

1 tablespoon chocolate chips

1 tablespoon sugar

Directions:

In a bowl, add milk, egg, brown sugar, cinnamon and vanilla extract and mix till well combined.
Stir in the raisins. In a baking dish, spread the bread cubes.
Pour milk mixture over bread cubes evenly.
Refrigerate for about 15-20 minutes.
Preheat the Airfryer to 375 degrees F.
Remove from refrigerator and sprinkle with chocolate chips and sugar.
Cook for about 12 minutes.

APPLE BREAD PUDDING

Time: 60 minutes   Servings: 8

Ingredients:

For Bread Pudding:

10½-ounce bread, cubed
½ cup apple, peeled, cored and chopped
½ cup raisins
¼ cup walnuts, chopped
1½ cups milk
¾ cup water
5 tablespoons honey

2 teaspoons ground cinnamon
2 teaspoons cornstarch
1 teaspoon vanilla extract

For Topping:

1 1/3 cups plain flour
3/5 cup brown sugar
7 tablespoons butter

Directions:

In a large bowl, mix together bread, apple, raisins and walnuts.
In another bowl, add remaining ingredients and mix till well combined.
Add milk mixture into bread mixture and mix till well combined.
Refrigerate for about 15 minutes, tossing occasionally.
For topping in a bowl, mix together flour and sugar.
With a pastry cutter, cut the butter and mix till a crumbly mixture forms.
Preheat the Airfryer to 355 degrees F.
Divide the mixture in 2 baking pans evenly.
Spread the topping mixture on top evenly.
Place 1 pan in an Airfryer basket.
Cook for about 22 minutes.
Repeat with the remaining pan

DOUGHNUTS PUDDING

Time: 80 minutes   Servings: 4

Ingredients:

6 glazed doughnuts, cut into small pieces
¾ cup frozen sweet cherries

½ cup raisins
½ cup semi-sweet chocolate baking chips

¼ cup sugar
1 teaspoon ground cinnamon

4 egg yolks
1½ cups whipping cream

Directions:

Line a baking dish with a piece of foil.

In a large bowl, mix together doughnut pieces, cherries, raisins, chocolate chips, sugar and cinnamon.

In another bowl, add egg yolks and whipping cream and beat till well combined.

Add the egg yolk mixture into doughnut mixture and mix well.

Place the doughnuts mixture into prepared baking dish evenly.

Preheat the Airfryer to 310 degrees F.

Place baking dish into Airfryer basket.

Cook for about 60 minutes.

Refrigerate to chill before serving

CREAM DOUGHNUTS

Time: 20 minutes

Servings: 8

Ingredients:

For Doughnuts:
½ cup sugar
2 tablespoons butter, softened
2 large egg yolks
2¼ cups plain flour
1½ teaspoons baking powder

1 teaspoon salt
½ cup sour cream
2 tablespoons butter, melted
For Topping:
1/3 cup caster sugar
1 teaspoon cinnamon

Directions:

In a bowl, add the sugar and softened butter and beat till creamy.

Add egg yolks and beat till well combined.

In another bowl, sift together flour, baking powder and salt.

Add 1/3 of the flour mixture and ½ of the sour cream in the bowl of sugar mixture and mix well.

Add remaining 1/3 of the flour and remaining sour cream and mix well.

Now, add the remaining flour and mix till a dough forms.

Refrigerate the dough before rolling.

Place the dough onto a lightly floured surface and roll into 2-inch thickness.

With a floured doughnut cutter, cut the dough.

Preheat the Airfryer to 355 degrees F.

Cot the both sides of the doughnuts with the melted butter.

Place the doughnuts in the Airfryer.

Cook for about 8 minutes or till golden brown.

Meanwhile in a bowl, mix together the topping ingredients.

Sprinkle the doughnuts with the cinnamon sugar and serve.

Milky Doughnuts

Time: 35 minutes   Servings: 12

Ingredients:

For Doughnuts:

1 cup all-purpose flour
1 cup whole wheat flour
2 teaspoons baking powder
Salt, to taste
¾ cup sugar
1 egg

1 tablespoon butter, softened
½ cup milk
2 teaspoons vanilla extract

For Glaze:

2 tablespoons icing sugar
2 tablespoons condensed milk
1 tablespoon cocoa powder

Directions:

In a bowl, mix together flours, baking powder and salt.
In another bowl, add sugar and egg and beat till fluffy and light.
Add the flour mixture in egg mixture and mix.
Add butter, milk and vanilla extract and mix till a soft dough forms.
Refrigerate the dough for at least 1 hour.
Place the dough onto a lightly floured surface and roll to ½-inch thickness.
With a small doughnut cutter, cut 24 small doughnuts from the rolled dough.
Preheat the Airfryer to 390 degrees F.
Place the doughnuts in an Airfryer basket in 3 batches.
Cook for about 6-8 minutes.
Remove from Airfryer and keep aside to cool completely.
Sprinkle with icing sugar.
In a bowl, mix together condensed milk and cocoa powder.
Spread the glaze over doughnuts and serve.

Fruity Tacos

Time: 15 minutes   Servings: 2

Ingredients:

2 soft shell tortillas
4 tablespoons strawberry jelly
¼ cup blueberries

¼ cup raspberries
2 tablespoons powdered sugar

Directions:

Preheat the air fryer at 300 degrees F.
Spread 2 tablespoons of strawberry jelly over each tortilla.
Top with blueberries and raspberries. Sprinkle with powdered sugar.
Place the tortillas in an Airfryer basket.
Cook for about 5 minutes until crispy.

*B*UTTER SHORTBREAD FINGERS

Time: 25 minutes   Servings: 10

Ingredients:
1/3 cup caster sugar   ¾ cup butter
1 2/3 cups plain flour

Directions:
In a bowl, mix together sugar and flour.
Add butter and mix till a smooth dough forms.
Cut the dough into 10 equal sized fingers.
With a fork, lightly prick the fingers.
Preheat the Airfryer to 355 degrees F.
Lightly, grease a baking sheet.
Arrange the fingers into prepared baking sheet.
Transfer the baking sheet in an Airfryer basket.
Cook for about 12 minutes.

*A*PPLE DUMPLINGS

Time: 35 minutes   Servings: 2

Ingredients:
2 sheets puff pastry   2 tablespoons raisins
2 small apples, peeled and cored   2 tablespoons butter, melted
1 tablespoon brown sugar

Directions:
In a bowl, mix together sugar and raisins.
Fill the core of each apple with raisins mixture.
Fold the pastry around the apple so it is fully covered.
Place the apple in the centre of each sheet and fold dough to cover the apple completely.
Pinch the edges to seal.
Preheat the Airfryer to 355 degrees F.
Place the dumplings in an Airfryer basket.
Cook for 25 minutes.

*S*WEET WONTONS

Time: 25 minutes   Servings: 12

Ingredients:
For Wonton Wrappers: 18-ounce cream cheese, softened
½ cup powdered sugar   1 teaspoon vanilla extract

1 Package of wonton wrappers
For Raspberry Syrup:
¼ cup water

¼ cup sugar
1 (12-ounce) package frozen raspberries
1 teaspoon vanilla extract

Directions:

For wrappers in a bowl, mix together sugar, cream cheese and vanilla extract.

Place a wonton wrapper on a work surface.

Place about 1 tablespoon of the cream cheese mixture in the center of each wrapper.

With wet fingers, fold the wrappers around the filling.

Pinch the edges to seal.

Preheat the air fryer to 350 degrees F.

Place the wonton wrappers in an Airfryer basket.

Cook for about 8 minutes.

Meanwhile for syrup in a skillet, add water, sugar, raspberries and vanilla on medium heat.

Cook, stirring continuously for about 5 minutes.

Transfer the mixture into food processor and blend until smooth.

Serve the wonton with the topping of raspberry syrup.

APPLE PASTRY

Time: 35 minutes   Servings: 8

Ingredients:

½ of apple, peeled, cored and chopped
1 teaspoon fresh orange zest, grated finely
½ tablespoon white sugar

½ teaspoon ground cinnamon
7.05-ounce prepared frozen puff pastry

Directions:

Preheat the Airfryerto390 degrees F.

In a bowl, mix together all ingredients except puff pastry.

Cut the pastry in 16 squares.

Place about a teaspoon of the apple mixture in the center of each square.

Fold each square into a triangle and press the edges slightly with wet fingers.

Then with a fork, press the edges firmly.

In an Airfryer basket, place the pastries in batches.

Cook for about 10 minutes.

BANANA PASTRY

Time: 25 minutes   Servings: 4

Ingredients:

1 puff pastry sheet
½ cup nutella
2 bananas, sliced

Directions:

Cut the pastry sheet into 4 equal squares.

Spread nutella on each square of pastry evenly.

Divide banana slices over nutella evenly.

Fold each square into a triangle and press the edges slightly with wet fingers.

Then with a fork, press the edges firmly.

Preheat the Airfryer to 375 degrees F.

Place the pastries in an Airfryer basket

Cook for about 10-12 minutes.

ARSHMALLOW PASTRIES

Time: 20 minutes   Servings: 4

Ingredients:

4 filo pastry sheets, thawed
2-ounce butter, melted
¼ cup chunky peanut butter

4 teaspoons marshmallow fluff
Pinch of salt

Directions:

Brush 1 sheet of filo with butter.

Place a second sheet of filo on top of first one and brush it with butter.

Repeat till all 4 sheets are used.

Cut the filo layers in 4 (3x12-inch strips).

Place 1 tablespoon of peanut butter and 1 teaspoon of marshmallow fluff on the underside of a strip of filo.

Fold the tip of the sheet over the filling to form a triangle.

Fold repeatedly in a zigzag manner till the filling is fully covered.

Preheat air fryer 360 degrees F.

Place the pastries into cooking basket.

Cook for about 3-5 minutes.

Sprinkle with a pinch of salt before serving.

APPLE TART

Time: 40 minutes   Servings: 2

Ingredients:

2½-ounce butter, chopped and divided
3 ½-ounce flour
1 egg yolk

1-ounce sugar
1 large apple, peeled, cored and cut into 12 wedges

Directions:

In a bowl, add half of the butter, flour and mix till a soft dough forms.

Place the dough onto a floured surface and roll to 5.90-inch round.

Preheat the Airfryer to 390 degrees F.

In a baking pan, place the remaining butter and sprinkle with sugar.

Top with apple wedges in a circular pattern.

Place the rolled dough over apple wedges and gently press along the edges of the pan.

Arrange the pan in an Airfryer basket.

Cook for about 25 minutes.

Serve hot.

CHOCOLATY BALLS

Time: 30 minutes   Servings: 8

Ingredients:
2 cups plain flour   1 teaspoon vanilla extract
2 tablespoons cocoa powder   ¾ cup chilled butter
½ cup icing sugar   ¼ cup chocolate, chopped into 8 chunks
Pinch of ground cinnamon

Directions:
Preheat the Airfryer to 355 degrees F.

In a bowl, mix together flour, icing sugar, cocoa powder, cinnamon and vanilla extract.

With a pastry cutter, cut the butter and mix till a smooth dough forms. Divide the dough into 8 equal balls.

Press 1 chocolate chunk in the center of each ball and cover with the dough completely.

Place the balls on a baking sheet. Preheat the Airfryer to 355 degrees F.

Place the baking sheet in an Airfryer basket.

Cook for about 8 minutes.

Now, set the Airfryer to 320 degrees F.

Cook for about 5 minutes more.

APPLE CRUMBLE

Time: 40 minutes   Servings: 4

Ingredients:
1 (14-ounce) can apple pie   7 tablespoons caster sugar
¼ cup butter, softened   Pinch of salt
9 tablespoons self-rising flour

Directions:
Preheat the Airfryer at 320 degrees F.

Lightly, grease a baking dish.

Place the apple pie in the prepared baking dish evenly.

In a bowl, add remaining ingredients and mix till a crumbly mixture forms.

Spread the mixture over apple pie evenly.

Arrange the baking dish in an Airfryer basket.

Cook for about 25 minutes.

Fruit Crumble

Time: 35 minutes   Servings: 4

Ingredients:

½ pound fresh apricots, pitted and cubed
1 cup fresh blackberries
1/3 cup sugar, divided
1 tablespoon fresh lemon juice

7/8 cup flour
Pinch of salt
1 tablespoon cold water
¼ cup chilled butter, cubed

Directions:

Preheat the Airfryer to 390 degrees F.

Grease a baking pan.

In a bowl, mix together apricots, blackberries, 2 tablespoons of sugar and lemon juice.

Spread apricot mixture in the prepared baking pan.

In a bowl, add remaining ingredients and mix till a crumbly mixture forms.

Spread the flour mixture over the apricot mixture evenly.

Place the pan in an Airfryer basket.

Cook for about 20 minutes.

Apple Pie

Time: 45 minutes   Servings: 6

Ingredients:

1 frozen pie crust, thawed
1 large apple, peeled, cored and chopped
3 tablespoons sugar, divided
1 tablespoon ground cinnamon

2 teaspoons fresh lemon juice
½ teaspoon vanilla extract
1 tablespoon butter, chopped
1 egg, beaten

Directions:

Grease a pie pan.

Cut 1 crust about 1/8-inch larger than pie pan.

Cut a second crust a little smaller than first one.

In the bottom of prepared pie pan, arrange the large crust.

In a bowl, add apple, 2 tablespoons of sugar, cinnamon, lemon juice and vanilla extract.

Transfer the apple mixture over the bottom crust evenly.

Place the chopped butter over apple mixture evenly.

Arrange the second crust on top and pinch the edges to seal.

Carefully, cut 3-4 slits in the top crust.

Spread the egg over top crust evenly and sprinkle with sugar.

Preheat the Airfryer at 320 degrees F.

Arrange the pan in an Airfryer basket.

Cook for about 30 minutes.

Pecan Pie

Time: 45 minutes   Servings: 6

Ingredients:

¾ cup brown sugar
¼ cup caster sugar
1/3 cup butter, melted
2 large eggs
1¾ tablespoons flour

1 tablespoon milk
1 teaspoon vanilla extract
1 cup pecan halves
1 frozen pie crust, thawed

Directions:

Preheat the Airfryer to 300 degrees F.
In a large bowl, mix together both sugars and butter.
Add eggs and beat till foamy.
Add flour, milk and vanilla extract and beat till well combined.
Fold in pecan halves.
In the bottom of prepared pie pan, arrange the crust.
Transfer the pecan mixture in pie crust evenly.
Arrange the pan in an Airfryer basket.
Cook for about 22 minutes.
Now, set the Airfryer at 285 degrees F.
Cook for about 13 minutes more.

Spiced Walnut Pie

Time: 45 minutes   Servings: 4

Ingredients:

1 (9-inch) prepared pie dough, store-bought or homemade, at room temperature
1 tablespoon unsalted butter
½ cup walnuts, chopped plus ¼-cup walnut halves
2 large eggs
¾ cup maple syrup

2 tablespoons light brown sugar
2 tablespoons almond butter
¾ teaspoon vanilla extract
½ teaspoon ground cinnamon
1/8 teaspoon ground nutmeg
Pinch of ground cloves
½ teaspoon salt

Directions:

Place the prepared pie dough onto a floured smooth surface. top.
Place an 8-inch plate face down on top of the pie dough and, using it as a template, cut around its edges to make an 8-inch pie shell.
Discard the extra dough.
Place the dough into a pie pan and fold the edges under itself.
In a small pan, add the butter and chopped walnuts on medium heat.
Cook for about 6-8 minutes, stirring occasionally.

Remove from the heat and place the walnuts mixture into the pie shell.

In a bowl, add the eggs, maple syrup, brown sugar, almond butter, vanilla extract, cinnamon, nutmeg and salt and beat till well combined.

Carefully pour the mixture over the toasted walnuts.

Top with the remaining walnut halves in a decorative pattern.

Preheat the Airfryer to 320 degrees F.

Place the pie an into Airfryer basket.

Cook for about to 25 minutes.

CHERRY PIE

Time: 35 minutes   Servings: 8

Ingredients:

2 refrigerated pre-made pie crusts   1 tablespoon milk
1 (21-ounce) can cherry pie filling   1 egg yolk

Directions:

Preheat the Airfryer to 320 degrees F.

Press one pie crust into a pie pan, removing excess hanging over.

With a fork, poke the holes all over dough

Place the pie pan into Airfryer basket.

Cook for about 5 minutes.

Remove pie pan from Airfryer basket.

Pour the cherry pie filling into pie crust.

Roll out the remaining pie crust and cut into ¾-inch strips

Place strips going one way across top and then the opposite way for a lattice pattern.

In a small bowl, add milk and egg and beat well.

Brush the top of pie with egg wash.

Place the pie pan into Airfryer basket.

Cook for about 15 minutes.

MINI PIES

Time: 50 minutes   Servings: 6

Ingredients:

For Crust: For Filling:

1½ cups flour   4 Granny Smith apples, peeled and
1 teaspoon sugar   chopped finely
Salt, to taste   1 teaspoon fresh lemon zest, grated finely
½ cup unsalted butter   2½ tablespoons sugar
¼ cup chilled water   2 tablespoons flour
                                          1 teaspoon ground cinnamon

¼ teaspoon ground nutmeg
Salt, to taste
¼ cup nutella
2 tablespoons fresh lemon juice
2 tablespoons butter

For Topping:
1 egg, beaten
3 tablespoons sugar
1 teaspoon ground cinnamon

Directions:

In a bowl, mix together butter, flour, sugar and salt.

With a pastry cutter, cut the butter in flour mixture.

Add chilled water and mix till a dough firms.

Transfer the dough into a bowl and cover with a plastic wrapper.

Refrigerate for about 30 minutes.

Meanwhile for filling in a bowl, mix together all ingredients except butter. Keep aside.

Place the dough onto a lightly floured surface and roll into about ½-inch thickness.

Press the ramekin in dough lightly and cut 12 circles.

Place 6 circles in the bottom of 6 ramekins and press slightly.

Place the filling mixture in the ramekins evenly and top with the remaining circles.

Pinch the edges to seal the pies.

Carefully, cut 3 slits in each pie and coat with beaten egg evenly.

For topping in a small bowl, mix together cinnamon and sugar.

Sprinkle with sugar mixture over each pie evenly.

Preheat the air fryer to 350 degrees F.

Arrange the pies in an Airfryer basket.

Cook for about 30 minutes.

SIMPLE CHEESECAKE

Time: 30 minutes

Servings: 12

Ingredients:

1 cup honey graham cracker crumbs
2 tablespoons unsalted butter, softened
1 pound cream cheese, softened

Sugar, to taste
2 large eggs
½ teaspoon vanilla extract

Directions:

Line a round baking dish with parchment paper.

For crust in a bowl, mix together graham cracker crumbs and butter.

Place the crust into baking dish and press to smooth.

Preheat the air fryer to 350 degrees F.

Place the baking dish in Airfryer basket.

Cook for about 4 minutes.

In bowl, add cream cheese and sugar and beat till smooth.

Add egg, one at a time and beat till mixture becomes creamy.

Add vanilla extract and mix well.

Remove the crust from air fryer.

Keep aside to cool slightly.

Place the cream cheese mixture in crust evenly.

Place the baking dish into Airfryer.

Cook for about15 minutes.

Refrigerate to chill for about 3 hours before serving.

PROTEIN CHEESECAKE

Time: 120 minutes   Servings: 10

Ingredients:

For Crust:

7 tablespoons almond flour

2 tablespoons natural peanut butter

1 tablespoon honey

For Filling:

2 eggs

10½-ounce fat-free plain Greek yogurt

10½-ounce fat-free cream cheese

2 scoops vanilla whey protein powder

2 tablespoons strawberry preserves

2 tablespoons splenda (sugar substitute)

¼ teaspoon vanilla extract

1 cup fresh strawberries, hulled and sliced

For Topping:

2 tablespoons fat-free plain Greek yogurt

1 tablespoon splenda (sugar substitute)

2 tablespoons vanilla whey protein powder

Directions:

Grease a round baking pan and then line with a parchment paper.

For crust in a bowl, add all ingredients and mix till a ball like dough forms.

Place the dough ball in the center of prepared baking pan.

With your fingers, press downwards till the dough spreads in the bottom of pan evenly.

Place the baking pan in an Airfryer basket.

Cook for about 7 minutes.

Meanwhile for filling in a large bowl, add all ingredients except strawberries and beat till smooth.

Fold in the strawberries.

Remove the crus from Airfryer.

Place the strawberry mixture over the crust evenly.

With the back of spatula, smooth the top surface of strawberry mixture.

Preheat the Airfryer to 245 degrees F.

Place the baking pan in an Airfryer basket.

Cook for about 30 minutes.

Now, set the Airfryer to 195 degrees F.

Cook for about 1 hour.

Remove from Airfryer and keep aside for about 1-2 hours to cool.

For topping in a bowl, mix together all ingredients

After cooling top the cheesecake with topping mixture evenly.

Refrigerate for about 4-8 hours before serving.

CHOCOLATE CHEESECAKE

Time: 45 minutes   Servings: 6

Ingredients:

3 eggs, separated
1 cup white chocolate, chopped
½ cup cream cheese, softened

2 tablespoons cocoa powder
2 tablespoons powdered sugar
¼ cup apricot jam

Directions:

In a bowl, add egg whites and refrigerate to chill before using.

In a microwave safe bowl, add chocolate and microwave on high for about 2 minutes, stirring after every 30 seconds. Add cream cheese and microwave for about 1-2 minutes or till cream cheese melts completely.

Remove from microwave and stir in egg yolks.

Remove egg whites from refrigerator and beat till firm peaks form.

Add 1/3 of the beaten egg whites in egg white mixture and mix.

Fold in remaining beaten egg whites.

Preheat the Airfryer at 285 degrees F.

Transfer the mixture into a cake pan.

Arrange the cake pan in an Airfryer basket.

Cook for about 30 minutes.

Remove from Airfryer and keep aside to cool completely.

Refrigerate to chill before serving.

Just before serving, dust with powdered sugar.

Spread jam on top evenly and serve.

BUTTER CAKE

Time: 35 minutes   Servings: 2

Ingredients:

3-ounce butter, softened
½ cup caster sugar
1 egg
1 1/3 cups plain flour, sifted

Pinch of salt
½ cup milk
Icing sugar to serve

Directions:

In a bowl add the butter and sugar and beat till light and creamy.

Add the egg and beat the till smooth and fluffy.

Add the flour and salt and mix well alternately with the milk.

Preheat your air fryer to 350 degrees F. Grease a small ringed cake pan with non-stick spray.

Transfer the mixture into the cake pan evenly.

Place the cake pan in Airfryer.

Cook for about 15 minutes or till a toothpick inserted into the center comes out cleanly.

8. Dust with icing sugar before serving.

$\mathcal{A}$PPLE $\textsc{Cake}$

Time: 55 minutes   Servings: 6

Ingredients:

1 cup all-purpose flour
1/3 cup brown sugar
1 teaspoon ground nutmeg
1 teaspoon ground cinnamon
½ teaspoon baking soda

Salt, to taste
1 egg
5 tablespoons plus 1 teaspoon vegetable oil
¾ teaspoon vanilla extract
2 cups apples, peeled, cored and chopped

Directions:

In a large bowl, mix together flour, sugar, spices, baking soda and salt.
In another bowl, add egg and oil and beat till smooth.
Add vanilla extract and beat well.
Slowly, add the flour mixture, beating continuously till well combined.
Fold in apples.
Preheat the Airfryer at 355 degrees F for about 5 minutes.
Transfer the mixture into a baking pan.
Cover with the foil paper and poke some holes with fork.
Place the baking pan in Airfryer and set the Airfryer to 320 degrees F.
Cook for about 40 minutes.
Remove the foil and cook for about 5 minutes more.
Cool completely and cut into slices.

$\mathcal{B}$ANANA $\textsc{Cake}$

Time: 35 minutes   Servings: 6

Ingredients:

1½ cups cake flour
1 teaspoon baking soda
½ teaspoon ground cinnamon
Salt, to taste
½ cup vegetable oil
2 eggs

½ cup sugar
½ teaspoon vanilla extract
3 medium bananas, peeled and mashed
¼ cup walnuts, chopped
¼ cup raisins, chopped

Directions:

Preheat the Airfryer at 320 degrees F.
Grease a 6-inch round baking pan.
In a large bowl, mix together flour, baking soda, cinnamon and salt.
In another bowl, add oil and egg and eat well.
Add sugar, vanilla extract and bananas and beat till well combined.
Transfer the mixture in the prepared pan.
Spread walnuts and raisin on top evenly.

Cover the pan with a foil paper.

Set the Airfryer to 300 degrees F.

Cook for about 30 minutes.

Remove the foil paper

Now, set the Airfryer at 285 degrees F.

Cook for about 5-10 minutes.

CHOCOLATE CAKE

Time: 65 minutes   Servings: 9

Ingredients:

For Cake:

1/3 cup plain flour

¼ teaspoon baking powder

1½ tablespoons unsweetened cocoa powder

2 egg yolks

½-ounce castor sugar

2 tablespoon vegetable oil

3¾ tablespoons milk

1 teaspoon vanilla extract

For Meringue:

2 egg whites

1-ounce castor sugar

1/8 teaspoon cream of tartar

Directions:

For cake in a large bowl, sift together flour, baking powder and cocoa powder.

In another bowl, add remaining ingredients and beat till well combined.

Add to flour mixture and beat till well combined.

For meringue in a large bowl, add all ingredients and beat on high speed till stiff peaks form.

Place 1/3 of the meringue and with hand beater, beat well.

Fold in the remaining meringue in cake mixture. Preheat the Airfryer to 355 degrees F.

Transfer the mixture into an ungreased chiffon pan. Cover the pan with the foil paper tightly.

With a fork, poke some holes in the foil paper. Set the Airfryer at 320 degrees F.

Cook for about 30 minutes. Remove the foil paper. Now, set the Airfryer at 285 degrees F.

Cook for about 35-38 minutes.

Remove foil and cook for about 5 minutes more.

Cool completely and cut into slices.

SEMOLINA CAKE

Time: 30 minutes   Servings: 8

Ingredients:

2½ cups semolina

½ cup vegetable oil

1 cup milk

1 cup plain Greek yogurt

1 cup sugar

½ teaspoon baking soda

1½ teaspoons baking powder

Pinch of salt

¼ cup raisins

¼ cup walnuts, chopped

Directions:

In a bowl, add semolina, oil, milk, yogurt and sugar and mix till well combined.

Cover and keep aside for about 15 minutes.

Add baking soda, baking powder and salt and mix till well combined.

Fold in raisins and walnuts.

Preheat the Airfryer to 390 degrees F.

Grease a baking pan.

Transfer the mixture into prepared baking pan.

Place the cake pan in Airfryer.

Now, set the Airfryer at 320 degrees F.

Cook for about 15 minutes.

LAYERED CAKE

Time: 40 minutes   Servings: 8

Ingredients:

For Cake:

3½-ounce plain flour
1 teaspoon ground cinnamon
Pinch of salt
7 tablespoons sugar
3½-ounce butter, softened
2 medium eggs

For Filling:

1¾-ounce butter, softened
1 tablespoon whipped cream
2/3 cup icing sugar
2 tablespoons strawberry jam

Directions:

In a large bowl, mix together flour, cinnamon and salt.

In another bowl, add sugar and butter and beat till creamy.

Add the eggs and beat till well combined.

Slowly, add flour mixture beating till well combined

Preheat the Airfryer to 355 degrees F.

Grease a cake pan.

Transfer the mixture into prepared cake pan.

Cook for about 15 minutes.

Now, set the Airfryer to 335 degrees F.

Cook for about 10 minutes.

Remove the cake from Airfryer and keep aside to cool completely.

After cooling, cut the cake in 2 portions.

For filling in a bowl, add the butter and beat till creamy.

Add cream and icing sugar and beat till a thick creamy mixture forms.

Place 1 cake portion in a plate, cut side up.

Spread jam over cake evenly and top with butter mixture.

Place another cake, cut side down over filling and serve.

LAVA CAKE

Time: 15 minutes   Servings: 6

Ingredients:

5 tablespoons sugar
2/3 cup unsalted butter
2 eggs
2/3 cup all-purpose flour

Salt, to taste
1 cup chocolate chips, melted
1/3 cup fresh raspberries

Directions:

Grease and 6 ramekins and dust with some sugar.

.

In a bowl, add sugar and butter and beat till creamy.
Add eggs and beat till fluffy.
Add chocolate mixture into egg mixture and beat well.
Add flour and salt and mix till well combined.
Fold in melted chocolate chips.
Preheat the Airfryer to 355 degrees F.
Transfer the mixture into prepared ramekins about ¾ full.
Place the ramekins in an Airfryer basket.
Cook for about 3 minutes.
Serve with the garnishing of raspberries.

RED VELVET CUPCAKES

Time: 30 minutes   Servings: 12

Ingredients:

For Cupcakes:

2 cups refined flour
¾ cup icing sugar
2 teaspoons beet powder
1 teaspoon cocoa powder
¾ cup peanut butter
3 eggs
¾ cup peanut butter
3 eggs

For Frosting:

¾ cup icing sugar
1 cup butter
1 cup cream cheese
¼ cup strawberry sauce
1 teaspoon vanilla essence

For Garnishing:
½ cup strawberries, hulled and sliced

Directions:

For cupcakes in a large bowl, add all ingredients and with electric beater, beat till well combined.
Transfer the mixture into silicon cups about 2/3 of full.
Preheat the Airfryer to 340 degrees F.
Place the cupcakes into an Airfryer basket.

Cook for about 10-12 minutes.

Transfer muffin tin onto a wire rack to cool completely.

Meanwhile for frosting in a bowl, add all ingredients and beat well.

Spread frosting over each cupcake evenly.

Garnish with strawberry slices and serve.

STRAWBERRY CUPCAKES

Time: 20 minutes   Servings: 12

Ingredients:

For Cupcakes:

½ cup caster sugar
7 tablespoons butter
2 eggs
½ teaspoon vanilla essence
7/8 cup self-rising flour

For Icing:

1 cup icing sugar
3½ tablespoons butter
1 tablespoon whipped cream
¼ cup fresh strawberries, blended
½ teaspoon pink food color

Directions:

Preheat the Airfryer to 340 degrees F.

In a bowl, add butter and sugar and beat till fluffy and light.

Add the eggs, one at a time and beat till well combined.

Stir in vanilla extract.

Slowly, add flour and beat till well combined.

Transfer the mixture into silicon cups.

Transfer the muffin tin into Airfryer basket.

Cook for about 8 minutes.

Transfer muffin tin to a wire rack to cool completely.

For toping in a bowl, add eat sugar and butter and beat till fluffy and light.

Add whipped cream, strawberries and color into mixture and mix till well combined.

Fill the pastry bag with icing and decorate the cupcakes.

CREAM CHEESE & RASPBERRY CUPCAKES

Time: 30 minutes   Servings: 10

Ingredients:

4 ½-ounce self-rising flour
½ teaspoon baking powder
Pinch of salt
½-ounce cream cheese, softened
4¾-ounce butter, softened

4¼-ounce caster sugar
2 eggs
2 teaspoons fresh lemon juice
¼ cup fresh raspberries

Directions:

In a bowl, mix together flour, baking powder and salt.

In another bowl, add cream cheese and butter and beat till smooth.

Add sugar and beat till fluffy and light.

Add eggs, one at a time and beat until just blended.

Add flour mixture into egg mixture and mix well.

Stir in lemon juice.

Transfer the mixture into 10 silicon cups.

Top each cup with 2 raspberries.

Preheat the Airfryer to 365 degrees F.

Place the silicon cups in an Airfryer basket.

Cook for about 20 minutes.

CHOCOLATE BROWNIES

Time: 35 minutes   Servings: 8

Ingredients:

½ cup chocolate, chopped roughly
1/3 cup butter
5 tablespoons sugar
1 large egg, beaten

1 teaspoon vanilla extract
Pinch of salt
5 tablespoons self-rising flour
¼ cup walnuts, chopped

Directions:

In a microwave safe bowl, add chocolate and butter and microwave on high for about 2 minutes, stirring after every 30 seconds.

Keep aside to cool.

In a bowl, add sugar, egg, vanilla extract and salt and beat till creamy and light.

Add chocolate mixture and beat till well combined.

Add flour and walnuts and mix till well combined.

Preheat the Airfryer to 355 degrees F.

Line a baking pan with greased parchment paper.

Transfer the mixture into prepared pan evenly.

With the back of spatula, smooth the top surface of mixture.

Place the pan in an Airfryer basket.

Cook for about 20 minutes.

Remove the baking pan from Airfryer and keep aside to cool completely.

Cut into 8 equal sized squares and serve.

Conclusion

If you're planning to feed on deep fried foods yet with zero or minimum fat then an air fryer is the best choice. The food is fried in air fryer is healthy and very low calorie. This amazing book gives you 365 recipes which makes a whole lot of 365 days of healthy eating. With these best tasting and healthy recipe you will be able to have complete grasp over air fryer cooking so you can customize your food to your choice afterwards.

Thank you again for purchasing this book!

Finally, if you enjoyed this book, please take the time to share your thoughts and post a review on Amazon. It'd be greatly appreciated!

Feel free to contact me at emma.katie@outlook.com

Check out more books by Emma Katie at:

www.amazon.com/author/emmakatie

Made in the USA
Lexington, KY
14 December 2018